I Love Being Abroad

. . . .

Memoirs of an
American Chanteuse in Paris

Dedicated to Stacy Ward Macadams
1938-2025
"Work the room, Jewel!"

. . . .

© 2025 Julie Cascioppo

Library of Congress Control Number: 2025906311

Contents

Prologue: Premonition 5
1. **Paris Will Love You!** 12
2. **Au Revoir, Seattle** 18
3. **Nightmare in the City of Light** 24
4. **I Love Paris in the Fall** 31
5. **Père-Lachaise** 39
6. **Unhinged Canadian Singer** 45
7. **Kindness of Strangers** 51
8. **Synchronicity in the Soap Suds** 55
9. **Gunila, Velkommen** 66
10. **Paying My Dues in Polka-Dot Shoes** 73
11. **American Church in Paris** 79
12. **Discovering the Hollywood Savoy** 83
13. **Claude the Moroccan** 92
14. **Lavelle** 96
15. **Getting to Be a Habit with Me** 99
16. **Madam Lenora** 102
17. **Tor Comes to Visit, Uh-Oh** 109

PHOTO GALLERY 116

(continued next page)

18. **Flirting with the Famous** *122*

19. **Everything Must Change** *125*

20. **Cocktail Party with a Famous Jazz Cat** *130*

21. **Decadence** *134*

22. **Panic on the Périphérique** *142*

23. **Norwegian Twins** *149*

24. **Rue Gît-le-Coeur** *155*

25. **Fontainebleau Fantasy** *162*

26. **New York Debut** *166*

27. **Defrosting the Cold War, on the Dance Floor** *173*

Epilogue *177*

Prologue: Premonition

If you bring forth what is within you, what you bring forth will save you. If you do not bring forth what is within you, what you do not bring forth will destroy you.
— Gospel of Thomas

MY BRILLIANT BROTHER NORMAN was the eldest child in the family, and I, the only girl, was four years younger. Norman took music seriously, rigorously studying classical piano at an early age. Later, in college, he made the esoteric choice to study classical organ. I was proud of how he poured himself passionately into any discipline he took on. Later, he returned to his first love, piano. With his free spirit and sensitivity, music seemed to bring out a strength and artfulness that felt divinely guided. I wondered if music could be his salvation.

As a young teenager (during those nowhere years when I felt both invisible and painfully conspicuous), I was curious about Norman's popular-music anthologies stashed carelessly among his extensive classical collection. I had little interest in classical music; there were usually no lyrics, and the musical notation might as well have been Swahili.

When he left his door unlocked, I'd spend hours sitting on the cold tile floor in his basement bedroom, leafing through his collection of songbooks. I was searching for something I might recognize that I could sing. Singing was soothing to me. I didn't feel it was "snooping" to want to be near him and uncover the secrets of my revered and mysterious brother.

I marveled at the incidental things he left haphazardly on a dresser or his desk—things he'd collected in his everyday life: snapshots of friends, small paperback books of Greek poetry, cuff links (What were those pretty things for?), a fountain pen, postcards from Europe. Fascinating mementos from experiences I had yet to have. He had refined tastes and specialized in collecting ceramics, photographs of famous opera singers and composers, and long-playing records by celebrated artists I had only heard of through him. Fascinated by the curios displayed in his room, I hoped he would not suddenly burst in and be angry to find me there. In our volatile family, respecting anyone's boundaries hadn't been enforced. (Though we did respect padlocks.)

When he was feeling generous or was bored with practicing, he'd manifest a Judy Garland songbook and encourage me to sing "Over the Rainbow," "On the Atchison, Topeka and the Santa Fe," or other selections from her movies.

Norman loved classical music, but he also surreptitiously appreciated popular standards. "A Taste of Honey" was one of the first "grown-up" songs I learned under his tutelage. He especially liked "Autumn Leaves" and taught me to sing it in French. At that time, I couldn't see the point of singing it in another language, but I learned it because if Norman suggested something, I knew it was worthwhile. He helped by writing it out phonetically. Later, I found singing in French and other Romance languages added an interesting element to my repertoire. When I started singing professionally, this opened doors for me and stimulated my aptitude for languages.

I was hungry to express myself musically—an example of having a passion yet not having access to a voice teacher who taught nonclassical singing. I didn't know such teachers even existed in Seattle. The prevailing thought was that if you learned classical music, then you could do anything you wanted, which is very far from the truth. I picked up music by listening to my parents' record collection and the radio's pop station, by singing in elementary school and church, and by my brother introducing it to me.

I wondered how singers learned to read the esoteric symbols on sheet music and bring a song to life. I imagined that it was beyond my abilities, and that if I succeeded it wouldn't be due to my talent but to my brother's introduction to it. There was some bigheartedness in his attempts to teach me basics, like the solfège method (do, re, mi . . .) of reading music, how to warm up my voice with scales, and a few Maria Callas arias.

But secretly I believed I might be stepping on his toes by being too interested in music. I knew this and tentatively proceeded in my own indirect way.

I loved it when Norman would take time out from his disciplined practice for some comic relief. He'd play selections from that big book of *Organ Favorites for Special Occasions*. "Roses and Lollipops" was a beloved choice that I related to. Both the melody and the words were easy for me. Same with "The Boy Next Door." He taught me the ones he liked, and soon I liked them as well.

As a classical musician, he didn't transpose songs into my key. At times, he laughed at me, and even I admit my voice sounded funny singing in a key that was totally wrong for me. When he was bored and through with this departure from his practicing, he'd say, "I have to practice now; your voice is giving me a headache." I didn't argue with him, as his playing in the wrong key for me was giving me a headache too.

Accepting his temperamental outbursts as his right, I would make a quick exit. I felt that ignoring his flare-ups would ensure more of his spontaneous master classes in the future. Unfortunately, his behavior sometimes made me assume, erroneously, that I couldn't sing. (Could he have been feeling competitive?) As much as I loved singing, I didn't dare admit that I was taking it seriously, and no one in my family encouraged it except at occasional holiday gatherings, when he would reluctantly play and I would sing. It was then that my singing more often became a platform for Norman to goof off and make fun of me, as I was "so bad." But I hung in there. At least I was getting some attention.

Despite his intermittent cruel humor, I felt I could learn things from him that I'd never learn from anyone else, which was not healthy in the long run. I learned I had to take abuse in order to get a little of something I desperately desired. Eventually, as I matured in high school, I would tag along with him and his friends to gay bars and drag shows at clandestine joints like the Golden Crown or Shelly's Leg, one of the infamous gay bars in Pioneer Square. Drag shows were my serendipitous education in dramatic, comedic performance. It was a lesson in creating over-the-top personas and tapping into a performer's connection to an audience by entertaining without inhibitions.

· · · · · · · · · · · · · · · · ·

Our home pulsated when Norman practiced Mozart sonatas, Beethoven concertos, Bach preludes . . . the list was endless. My favorites were his dreamy interpretations of Chopin. It was one thing my parents didn't seem to mind. Or maybe that was why they drank?

In his teen years Norman had his share of troubles with the kids in the neighborhood. He was different from the others, although I never saw him that way. It's interesting what you don't notice when you admire someone. I sensed he was gay, but no one spoke of it or knew precisely what that was—and why it was a problem. It seemed a nonissue to me. There was an underlying, subtle tension in our home toward him, stemming from that unspoken topic.

In our surrounding neighborhood, there were several edgy juvenile delinquents around Norman's age. When he was sixteen, this mob of thugs harassed him regularly on his way home from school. They followed him to find out where he lived, hoping to gang up on him.

For me, his adoring twelve-year-old sister, witnessing this was eerie and disturbing. I watched in awe from the large living room window as this group of hoods leaned against our dad's meat truck, chanting, "Norman! Norman! Norman!" Each one held a water balloon ominously poised to be thrown at my brother.

Our mother, who never took crap from anyone, especially when it came to picking on her kids, went out on the porch, slamming open the metal screen door. She yelled in her surprisingly deep, smoky, masculine-timbre voice, "Get the hell off our property or I'll call the police and have you sent to reform school!"

They knew she meant it—or worse—as she walked threateningly down the steps, grabbing hold of a rusty rake leaning against our house to wield as a lethal weapon. They sensed she was capable of anything.

I loved her for that uninhibited way of yelling, and she meant business. (Maybe that's how I developed my commanding voice!) I was glad the bullies were on the receiving end of her wrath for a change, and not me.

Because of Norman's acute creativity and originality, I didn't take into account all the pain he experienced at school. He hid that from everyone. It was a treat for me to hang out with him, and at times I preferred my brother's company over that of my own friends. He and I spent endless hours improvising and recording self-generated psychodrama musicals based on our alcohol-fueled parents and relatives and their peculiar, boozy friends. Our "plays," as we called them, were based on movies we'd seen at the Grand Theatre, especially Boris Karloff horror films. After tape-recording them, we'd listen and laugh till we cried.

Sometimes our parents stopped in to see what we were up to, commenting, "You kids are nuts; you can get into trouble for doing that!" (As if there was a special police squad on the prowl for nutty kids.) They tried to hide their enjoyment, but they had a love of satirical comedy. As a family, the one thing we enjoyed, besides sharing delicious meals, was listening to records by genius comics like Jonathan Winters, Phyllis Diller, and Lily Tomlin and laughing together. Ah, to be young and overflowing with imaginative mischief! What a satisfying, dangerous thrill. I wonder what might have happened had Norman and I seriously gone into comedy together.

Norman found regular employment as a musician in churches and occasionally participated in concerts, recitals, and competitions. When I got my driver's license I gladly became Norman's chauffeur. Norman didn't get his until years later. I'd hang out at the church while he practiced, and then bring him home. It was around that time that I started examining the way I used my time. It needled me that I didn't have a passion to pour myself into as well.

One of the benefits of hanging around the church was I began to occasionally sing Lutheran solos, under his encouraging tutelage—like "Were You There When They Crucified My Lord?" He directed me to turn and gaze at the large cross, dramatizing the crucifixion. I also delivered a morbidly theatrical rendition of "The Old Rugged Cross." And I sometimes got paid.

Everyday life was unpredictably entertaining growing up, with daily opportunities for domestic drama. Norman was the instigator and I was the malleable fledgling actress—the drag queen he was afraid to be.

At seventeen, a senior in high school, I'd finally been on one of my first real dates with a guy whom I had a shy crush on. That year, I had blossomed (gratefully) into a young Maria Callas look-alike.

Norman, now twenty-one and attending the university, was majoring in piano, exploring new forms of expression, and exuding a noticeable confidence and panache.

I was envious that my brother and Matthew Kangas, his eccentric and equally nerdy friend since grade school, were often doing creative, fun projects without me, like making home movies or writing plays and performing them for the community in the Kangases' backyard. Matthew's mother doted on her two unconventional sons, encouraging all imaginative endeavors. This included the delegation of Matthew's younger brother, David, to play the unsavory roles—such as prisoner, crazy person, and slave. I was hurt that they didn't include me, although I was fully occupied doing summer stock at Green Lake's Bathhouse Theater.

On one particular night, Matthew (who eventually became a well-known art critic) and my brother held a mock nightclub show in Matthew's family's rec room, where he and Norman had been secretly rehearsing for weeks. I was invited and encouraged to bring my new "boyfriend."

Matthew played piano and Norman sang classic jazz numbers! This was something new. I hadn't ever heard him sing seriously before. His tone was deep, warm, whimsical, and sophisticated. He utilized a half-talking, half-singing style. It mesmerized me as it revealed a side of Norman that I had no idea existed.

But, most importantly, *something about me* was born that night that shook my world. More than a pleasant surprise, I had a realization: *I MUST do this!*

I accepted that Norman's preference for classical music was somehow superior to my love of popular song and jazz. Classical was the only thing he would ever want to perform in public. Yet he rendered jazz standards *impeccably*, with a style unlike any singer I've heard since.

The nightclub act in progress hadn't been mentioned before my seeing it, which made it all the more riveting. The night of that performance, in my mind the Kangas basement transformed into an actual nightclub. The mystique and professionalism of my brother and his friend ignited my fantasy-driven essence. Witnessing Norman's blossoming captivated my younger self completely!

Norman sat casually on a high stool, trim and fit, wearing fashionable hip-hugger bell-bottoms and a dreamy blue knit shirt, opened at the chest. This new Norman was a version of him never before seen. It seemed like he had stepped through a portal into his grander, more accessible self. No longer the focused, classical misfit, now he was sophisticated, impeccable, with a smooth mouthful of polished, jazzy innuendos!

He interpreted hip jazz tunes with such élan and showmanship that I was hypnotized. I watched with studious intensity. His persona that night, which he used as a "lark," alchemized into what had imperatively been missing in me. Now I had the specific role model I needed, and it was divinely becoming my own in that moment. That night was an epiphany that headed straight to my psyche.

What really got me was his ability to command the focus of the whole room. I paid attention because I wanted what he had; in fact, I knew I had it, I just had to get busy and start revealing it, never imagining that I might be stepping on his toes.

I fell under the enchantment of a muse as he sang "You're Getting to Be a Habit with Me," "Just One of Those Things," "What Are You Doing the Rest of Your Life?," "Once Upon a Time," and "Close Your Eyes."

I clung to every lyric, every understated double entendre, intoxicated with the energy of Norman's warm, mischievous talk-singing.

The seeds were sown. I surrendered completely to this unrealized dream.

When I spoke of that performance years later Matthew dramatically bellowed at me, "And Norman will NEVER FORGIVE YOU FOR THAT!" I had no idea that was the direction Norman hoped to explore.

Matthew implied that I stole Norman's dream! I thought Norman's dream was the piano and, later, the classical organ.

I needed a dream, damn it! The dream knew it as well and took me over, knocked me senseless, and captured me completely—right there in the Kangas basement. And it has never let me go.

1. Paris Will Love You!

. . . .

A solitary fantasy can create many realities.
— Maya Angelou

O**UT OF THE BLUE ON A SUNNY SEATTLE** afternoon in 1983, my reserved Norwegian boyfriend—a man of few words and big ideas—announced, "I've been wanting to remodel the kitchen. In order to not bother you, I was thinking of sending you to Paris for the month of October."

"Paris? That sounds utterly ridiculous, and fantastic, but seriously, what am I gonna do there?" I asked. Tor was in awe of my burgeoning singing talent and seemed to take it more seriously than I did.

"You know, you'll sign up for French class, discover Paris, and get some singing engagements at the cool clubs in Paris," said the man who would be footing most of the bill for this adventure.

Tor had spent time in Paris; he loved visiting the Cinémathèque Française and spending endless days and nights in dark theaters watching films. He imagined I would find Paris a beguiling city, where I could exercise both my historical curiosity and my desire to perform.

Secretly afraid of change, I teased, "How am I going to pull that off?" I was tempted to talk him out of it, but held my tongue, letting the offer marinate. Over the course of the next few weeks, it captured my imagination. I wanted to go—partly because it sounded exciting to everyone I mentioned it to—but I was terrified. No one I knew in 1980s

Seattle just up and went to Paris alone on a quest for singing gigs.

I'd been singing semiprofessionally since I was seventeen and was almost comfortable calling myself "a singer." Majoring in theater and music helped smooth out the rough edges. Beneath it all, I leaned more toward being a natural comedienne and actress.

After graduating from college in 1977, I'd sung off and on—at bars, art parties, and other events throughout Seattle, with a six-month stint in San Francisco cocktail lounges.

I studied with an expensive vocal coach who told me I could not call myself a jazz singer: "Until you know every sharp and flatted note in the key signature of the song you're singing, you're not a real jazz singer. When it comes to jazz, you better have your act together!"

True, I thought, *but I'm beyond jazz: I do everything!* Maybe I couldn't name the flats and sharps, but I could sing them.

Just months before, in February 1983, Tor and I had taken a glamorous Caribbean vacation, to the island of Saint Martin. It had been my first exotic trip outside the United States. We first flew to Miami, where we had an afternoon layover on the beach. After the bitter cold and rain of February in Seattle, it was a wonder to behold Miami Beach and the Atlantic, idyllically passing a few hours before our 1,200-mile flight to the island of Saint Martin.

The Miami airport was teeming with colorful, vibrant people from wild and wonderful South American places where they smiled at each other and seemed to mean it. I hoped it was a good omen embarking on an intriguing, colorful, off-the-beaten-track vacation. Refreshed and anticipating our adventure, we boarded a small jet for Saint Martin. Tor insisted I take the window seat.

"Won't I block your view?" I asked demurely. I'd never traveled with a man before. Tor was my first serious boyfriend.

"No, you enhance it," he replied. "I get to see you first, and then I might look at the view."

Really? I thought. Wow, no one had ever said something so sweet to me.

Tor had been an avid world traveler before I knew him, and he enjoyed visiting tropical places after spending a season as a commercial fisherman in the frigid Bering Sea. He introduced me to the enchantments of exotic travel. This was our second winter together. We had gone on the Atkins diet and each lost twelve pounds. We were svelte and ready to enjoy a real vacation—swimming, rubbing shoulders with glamorous folk, trying new foods, and enjoying the music and culture of a faraway paradise. Catapulted out of the dank Seattle winter into the equatorial sunlight of the Caribbean, I felt another side of my personality rise. The lightness and warmth of the air stirred something deep within me.

I felt an overwhelming appreciation of the strange, new faces; the tropical change of scenery; and the clear, sparkling waters.

On our first night at La Samanna, a luxurious resort hotel on the French side of Saint Martin, we became friendly with two fellow guests, the inquisitive Michel and his handsome father, Guy. They were Frenchmen who had come from Paris to sell jewelry to high-end boutique hotels and shops on the island. During the sultry evening, under a full moon, we gathered around the bar by the pool to enjoy the polished grooves of a local Calypso band. When I casually mentioned that I was a singer back in Seattle, Michel surprised me by demanding, "Sing now! There is a band, the moon is full, and we're all so young!"

The combo had an easygoing vibe, and Michel had a way of refusing to take no for an answer. In that moment, his manner seemed endearing, and since we were there on vacation, acquiescing to his request seemed like a good way to break the ice. He rushed to the stage to arrange my Caribbean debut.

As we were on the French side of the island, I suggested the well-known torch song "La Vie en Rose." The band launched into a seductive bossa nova rhythm, à la Grace Jones. Approaching the bandstand in gladiator sandals and a white cotton beach dress, I felt underdressed and unprepared. But as I delivered the well-honed French lyrics, I was swept up in the music; there, under the moon on the other side of the world, I sang from my heart.

I felt the usual self-conscious shyness after my performance, but as the small audience applauded warmly, Michel stood, clapping louder than anyone, and grinned, announcing, "YOU must come to Paris and sing! Paris will love you!" His father smiled and nodded as he sipped his cognac. Tor agreed enthusiastically as well.

Michel added, "When you come to Paris, I'll pick you up at the airport and introduce you to important people in the music business!" I was flattered by the extravagant praise from the French chaps and a blushing Tor. Paris as a vacation destination was appealing but out of my reach. Also, finding a singing engagement in any foreign country was beyond me. It was hard enough landing gigs in Seattle, where I spoke the language.

La Samanna was frequented by jet-setters and glamorous rock-star types.

Antonio, a hotel bartender who had befriended us, offered to take us to an "authentic" hot spot with music and dancing, popular with the locals. We took his funky car. The clientele at this "authentic club" consisted of island natives dressed in their colorful dance attire. They paid no attention to us as foreigners. Tor declined to dance, so Antonio invited me to dance with him and showed me some "island moves." The music was electrifying, as the dancers wildly descended into dance mania.

Tor's usual calm and stoic appearance changed as the night unfolded. His increasingly furrowed brow revealed he was made uncomfortable by the lively Dionysian celebration. Unless pushed beyond his limits, Tor was usually a gentle introvert. We invited him to join in, but he refused. When I tried to cajole him into participating, he pushed me away and went outside to be alone. Antonio, noticing Tor's reaction, offered to take us back to the hotel.

Perhaps he felt threatened by my flamboyant expressive antics—I had combined old dances like the boogaloo and Watusi and threw in a few high kicks. Then everyone participated in what looked like a dance called "the Human Chain." I enjoyed what felt like fun moments of expressing my true self. I yearned to be a performer and an actress who did what she liked. I could see that Tor was shy and embarrassed witnessing interactions that I thought were helping me develop my persona as a performer.

The next morning over breakfast, he and I laughed together, somewhat cautiously, about his churlish exit the previous evening. Tor chuckled, "It was funny, that look on Antonio's face, when he hurried to take us back to the hotel!"

Despite that setback, Tor and I grew closer and had a wonderful vacation, with breakfasts by the pool—freshly baked croissants and delicious cafés au lait—going for swims in the healing waters of the Caribbean, reading and luxuriating on its white sandy beaches. When we returned to Seattle, I realized that the Saint Martin experience had awakened in me a desire for something more. I kept professionally in touch with Michel, our French friend from the hotel—I had my career to focus on.

Tor returned to fishing in the spring and summer. When he returned to Seattle, he had been home for a week, working on numerous upgrade projects for the house, when he brought up the sentimental memories of La Samanna and how well received I had been there, singing for the French visitors.

Our life in Seattle was unusually comfortable, sweet, and predictable—safe. We had Sophie, our beloved Australian shepherd—I had given her as a puppy to Tor for Christmas. He had been an only child and had never had a dog before. She and I were a good team for Tor. Returning to the potential Paris adventure that Tor had sprung on me, I was charmed as well as reluctant, but I knew I wanted something more. One clear night in September, I gazed up at the autumn night sky and felt that, given all the doubts and questions rampaging through my imagination, I might as well be considering a trip to the moon.

Tor believed in me more than I did. He often reminded me that, with my talents, I could become a success. I truly loved singing and felt I had it in me to be a professional, but when it came to the question of doing it in a foreign culture, I balked, unconvinced that I could handle it. For starters, I had only completed one relevant language course, French for Tourists.

"You have more ability to become rich and famous than I do," asserted Tor.

His mind was made up—he would remodel the kitchen, and I would go to Paris. At some point, I stopped overanalyzing his suggestion and saw it as a once-in-a-lifetime opportunity. After all, everyone has to go to Europe at some time. Once I was there, I could adapt. After all, I had spent two quarters in Mexico during my freshman year of college. I was good with Romance languages once I got the hang of conjugating verbs. And everybody loves a singer. If things got rocky, I'd break into "Summertime"!

Tor let me know the remodel might take more than a month. He was not sure when he'd finish, so I was soon in possession of a round-trip ticket with a flexible return date.

With Tor standing by offering moral support, for the first time in my life I picked up the phone and reserved a place to stay in Europe—Hôtel Odéon in the heart of Saint-Germain-des-Prés (so mysterious sounding).

I planned to sign up at the Alliance Française for French lessons as soon as I arrived and then hit the streets to check out the music scene. I was somewhat confident about looking for singing engagements. I'd been doing that forever, although in English. I had a professional demo tape, a résumé, some dramatic publicity photos, and a suitcase full of sheet music.

In Seattle I'd been singing around the lounge circuit and appeared regularly at the popular Pink Door Cabaret, performing with the great pianist and collaborator Ben Fleck several nights a week. I had become known as a "one-woman show." While singing jazz, show tunes, and blues, I started feeling comfortable changing things up by adding comedic characters. My performances were a combination of lounge, vaudeville, and comedy act delivered by an assortment of original characters that were all me acting out different ludicrous careers. (If you can't actually get a job in the career you want, just make fun of it.)

My act was well received by locals and tourists. I wasn't sure if I was on the right track, but I was having fun exploring that element of performing and developing my stage presence with an audience.

Now, on my way to Paris, in October 1983, it was time again to explore unknown facets of my talent and other venues and possibilities. Friends and fans frequently offered career advice—new songs to perform, or "What about going to New York . . . LA . . . Vegas?" or "You should be on television!" My mind was spinning at the thought of trying and doing everything people suggested. I needed to narrow the options. I wanted to concentrate on singing, and Paris might just be the place where that's all I could do.

2. Au Revoir, Seattle

....

"Do something radical, now!"
— Unknown

RELIEVED TO BE ON MY WAY TO PARIS after the chaotic months of preparation, I reclined into my comfy airline seat. Sipping my complimentary champagne, I silently thanked my brother Norman for wrangling a first-class upgrade for me from his friend Jerry, an often-inebriated ticket agent for British Airways.

Relaxing into the long flight ahead, my mind wandered back to the events of my final hours in Seattle. They seemed to signal that Paris was what my burgeoning career and lifestyle needed.

For instance, one afternoon in October, less than a week before I was to depart for Paris, the telephone's insistent ring cut through my cloudy thoughts, startling me out of my confusion over what shoes to pack for my upcoming trip. I'd been making sporadic attempts at packing for months, hindered by bouts of indecision, even about going on this journey, so an interruption was welcome.

"Bonjour," I answered, with a French accent.

The voice at the other end replied brusquely with the last response I could imagine.

"This is the FBI calling for Julie Cash-o-po?" I paused, to decipher if the breathing style was that of my practical jokester brother.

I went along with it as a joke, despite my apprehension.

"The FBI? Now, what have I done? Norman, get serious, don't you get tired of making these crank calls? I'm packing." I laughed despite my annoyance. He was so creatively funny, I stopped what I was doing whenever he called.

Norman was the one person who never failed to make my life seem like a hilarious sitcom. I imagined his pretending to be the FBI was an affectionate way of saying goodbye to his adventurous younger sister whom he loved to laugh with and at. Somewhere along the line, that had become his only form of communicating with me.

"Good try, Norman, but I'm busy right now" (something I rarely said to him). "I'm packing my valise as we speak," I said with my recently acquired fake French accent.

(Throat clearing.) "This is the FBI and we'd like to question you regarding your association with the Russians you've been working with at the Seattle-based company Fish Resolutions since the spring of '83."

Uff da, this was no prank call. The FBI was searching for info about the visiting Russian vice president of the fishing company where I had, up until last week, worked as the part-time international telex operator.

The female employees in our office had been cautioned to stay "detached" from the visiting Russian. He was a "known provocateur" and any fraternizing could be grounds for dismissal. In retrospect I'm embarrassed to admit it, but my interest was immediately piqued. Back in the 1980s if someone had the slightest accent, I had to know them. I'd never met a "known provocateur."

I couldn't help myself. I was half Sicilian, half Norwegian, and unbridled hospitality was imprinted in my genetic makeup. Friends who knew this called me a one-woman welcome wagon. I had to get to know this mystery family, as I heard they were friendly, foreign, and lonesome. My kinda people.

The impatient-sounding agent wanted to know if anything subversive might be transpiring with the Russians that I could share with the FBI.

With his wife and child in tow, Igor, the Russian provocateur, had been in Seattle for five months to oversee the Soviet Union's interests in the purchase of a certain plentiful fish that Americans found unpalatable and that the Soviets were willing to buy.

While I was getting to know this unusual family around the office, their eight-year-old child, Nadia, who was the most precocious of the bunch, fell in love with me as only an eight-year-old girl coming from the repressed Soviet Union could.

"Why do you wear so much lipstick, Julia?" she would ask, mesmerized by my frequent applications.

"It just looks so good, honey." Not having a child of my own, I took pleasure in sharing valuable beauty secrets. She liked holding my hand rather than that of her stoic Polish mama, who spoke no English and wore no lipstick.

I accepted their friendly invitation to drop by their apartment. Since my trip to France was in the works, I felt there wouldn't be an issue about me "fraternizing."

At their apartment, before any provocative conversation could happen, Igor insisted on my tasting several different cognacs that had just arrived in a large, mysterious package from the Soviet Union via Washington, DC. His stoic wife seemed to roll her eyes as she sipped from a miniature glass, and he gulped, swallowed, and immediately poured another round, proving his alliance to the Russian spirit. For about an hour we savored the varieties of Russian cognac and other black-market delicacies from the Soviet Union, like sturgeon caviar, smoked eels, and a waxy, flavorless chocolate. We completed the tasting with strong, hand-rolled Russian cigarettes, often smoked by the Soviet fishermen. Over the next few weeks I made a number of visits and excursions with this Russian family, sometimes accompanied by Tor. On the phone, the FBI agent then cut to the chase. "We need to speak to you in person."

"Well, golly, I'm actually in the middle of packing and about to leave the country, nearly immediately," I explained professionally.

"You should come down now." His concerned delivery added to my curiosity.

Could something have happened to Igor and his family? How could this surreal phone call have anything to do with me? Especially hours before my departure? I wanted to call Tor, to whom I was currently almost engaged, and ask him what to do. Being fluent in Russian, Tor had welcomed the Soviet family as much as I. But this was before cell phones, and he was at a film and hadn't disclosed where. Not knowing what else to do, or who to call about this kerfuffle, in fifteen minutes I was entering a concrete building near Pioneer Square that I'd driven by all my life, never knowing this monolith was the home of the FBI.

Within moments I was ushered into the agent's office.

"It appears you are popular with the Soviets." He smiled menacingly.

My palms began to sweat as he pointed to a hard-back chair. I wondered how they got my number.

I reminded myself to remain calm, collected, and ready for Paris.

"Did you know that when you took the Soviets to Whidbey Island, you passed a top-secret Boeing facility that the Soviets are forbidden to be within ten miles of?" I had almost forgotten that I had taken them to Whidbey on an outing one Sunday.

"I believe I was confused and took a wrong exit off the freeway thinking it was the way to the ferry. We did not stop and at all times remained in the car."

"Are you interested in assisting the FBI in acquiring more information on these Soviets?"

I hadn't watched enough James Bond movies to know how to navigate this proposal. Was he insinuating I become a spy? There was no mention of it being a paid position—how much do spies make these days? And if they were asking me to work for them for free, well, what had the FBI ever done for me?

I let the agent know my contact with this family was friendly and superficial. I had to get home. "If something comes to mind, I'll give a call," I concluded.

Thank God the agent didn't press me for more information.

He thanked me for my time, and as I was about to disappear, he said, "We'd really appreciate any information. And I mean any. Call me when you're back in Seattle."

My fear of going to Paris evaporated, as a more menacing apprehension popped up if I remained. The waters felt like they could easily get deep, fast.

I had a ticket to Paris, a hotel reservation, and a suitcase of music to see me through a singing career.

. . . .

The hum of the jet engines soothed my frayed nerves and I began to feel drowsy. The passenger across from me glanced my way through rings of smoke.

"Would you care for a cigarette?"

"No thanks, I'm a singer."

"Are you going to Paris?"

"Well . . . isn't everybody on this plane going to Paris? Do people take airplanes to places they're not going to?" I said, attempting to sound more sophisticated and acerbic than I felt. I was on the edge of falling into a daydream. I wanted to bask in the lucky break of being whisked off to some unknown place, where I would get to magically reinvent my life for a whole month.

He chuckled, "Yes, we often transfer to another flight when we get to Paris. I'm on my way to Lebanon—have you been?" He smiled, showing great pride in that country.

"This is my first trip to Europe, but I've heard fascinating things about Lebanon," I said, recalling one of my and Tor's favorite Lebanese restaurants in Seattle.

Tor had thrown me a lavish bon voyage party the night before my departure, which had sounded like a great idea at the time. Our home was fantastically filled with friends and family showing bittersweet emotion about my leaving, while wishing me safe travels. I promised to send postcards and be home soon.

I don't recommend having a party the night before a major trip. At the party, Tor, atypically, drank much more than usual, and in a small alcove of the house, away from the guests, he told me that my leaving was finally hitting him. He started to sway, leaned forward, and fell with a loud thump. I had never seen him lose his equilibrium before, and I wasn't sure how our relationship would stand this kind of separation. I wanted it to work, but, with Tor's prompting and support, this trip to Paris was setting in motion what felt like a possible metamorphosis.

As I dozed off in my seat, my heart was sad to be letting go of all I had, but I reminded myself, it was just one month.

I thought of the Soviet family and how they were unable to attend my party. I would miss them as well. It struck me that I was leaving all my reliable and interesting relationships behind for something that had vaguely to do with my singing career.

I was now fully on a trajectory that might as well have been taking me to the moon.

3. Nightmare in the City of Light

True success is figuring out your life so you never have to be around jerks. — John Waters

SADLY, IT WAS MICHEL, NOT HIS HANDSOME FATHER, who offered to pick me up at the Charles de Gaulle Airport in Paris at 7:00 p.m.

Michel and I didn't have much in common, although it was his shouting, "Paris will love you!" at the bar in Saint Martin when I sang "La Vie en Rose" that got the ball rolling for me to actually be on this trip. He also generously offered to be my guide when I first arrived in Paris, in early October 1983.

Michel was a bit younger than I, a chubby and arrogant know-it-all with a young, undeveloped soul and greasy hair that fell in his eyes. He was nothing like his charming father, Guy, the kind of French man who got even more attractive with age.

It was intimidating to land in a large European city where I didn't know another soul except for Michel, though I'd been given several names and phone numbers from friends in Seattle—including Mia, the sister of a fellow student in my French class in Seattle.

Bleary-eyed, I found the passenger pickup area, where I spied Michel. For a brief second I rejoiced, recognizing his childlike moon face. He looked like he'd slimmed down, and his eyes were aglow.

"*Bonsoir, Julie! Ça va?*" He pulled me close and kissed me twice—

which I wasn't exactly prepared for. What did that mean?

"Bonjour, Michel. Merci pour arriver en temps!" I laughed at my attempt to speak rudimentary French.

Since it was 7:00 p.m. Paris time, Michel had an evening planned. After cramming my luggage into his compact car, he chimed, "Now I will show you my Paris!" And pointing to my bulging suitcases, he added, "As well as show you how to pack a suitcase properly, ha!"

Squeamishly, I felt we were embarking on a Two for the Road kind of honeymoon road trip, which was jarring. I was operating on limited reserves after the longest transcontinental flight of my life. As kind as his offer seemed, I was not up for any high jinks.

"I'm so tired I've been hallucinating," I replied. "I want to go to my hotel." I imagined he'd be sympathetic, as he spoke English fluently.

"Oh, Julie! You do not quite understand jet lag, do you? Everyone knows you must stay up *late* tonight, so that tomorrow you will be on French time!"

He made it sound so *facile* and refused to accept no as my answer. I gave in to be "polite." "OK, show me the Sacré-Coeur."

"Oui, mais, non. Not right now. First I'll take you to l'Arc de Triomphe, then Place de Vendôme and the Champs-Élysées . . . then—for dinner, so you will never forget! We will go to Montmartre, near zee Sacré-Coeur."

"Dinner?" I was flabbergasted. I'd just had breakfast on British Airways before changing planes in London. "Michel, it's impossible to go to a restaurant, I'm exhausted. Let's do it another time."

All I wanted was a hot bath, a big bed, and no visitors. (Unless it was his father coming to take Michel away.)

"Mais non, Julie. I've made reservations at a restaurant that is the oldest, most famous in all of Paris! So, you can never forget this first night as your introduction to the *real* Paris."

I was losing my equilibrium due to his insistence, by being polite. In retrospect, he was a boor who did not care about my wishes—or probably anyone's. As I reflect on that night, I realize that I had met these kinds of men before. Men who wanted to have things their way. They made me want to push them around and have things my way. Normally, I avoided such miscreants, but more often than not, I'd find myself in these awful situations that were difficult to get out of. I later understood that this was why I had to come to Paris alone. My lesson was to value my life and my time, by establishing my priorities.

After a convoluted drive up and down Paris for the first time, I barely had the strength to look out the window amid his shouting.

"Julie, you *must* look at this, it's world-class! It's iconic! There's nothing like this in America!"

I was numb with fatigue and wished this troubled soul would stop demanding my attention.

Slowly his car sputtered around winding, cobblestone streets passing ancient, fairy-tale-like apartment buildings. I noticed tourists taking photos of the city from the top of Montmartre. Reveling in the splendor of the Sacré-Coeur, I had a sudden feeling of joy and the promise that this landmark was nearing the end of my expedition with this idiot. (Despite this ordeal, the Sacré-Coeur would become one of my favorite churches in Paris.)

"Julie, nous sommes arrivés! Allons-y," he ordered as I crawled out of the car like a zombie. I was impressed by the surroundings but barely verbal. I tried to keep my spirits up and play along with this tour of Paris.

As if in a bizarre dream, I felt like an exhausted carnival donkey on the brink of collapse. Yet still, the entitled child insisted, "One more ride around the pony pen!" I was beginning to lose hope that this evening would end. I reminded myself I was here to reinvent myself, to explore the potential of a French audience, and to see if visiting Paris could bring me to another level of sophistication and worldliness.

We sat at a sidewalk table outside the restaurant in Montmartre. It was reminiscent of the Utrillo prints with which my mother had decorated our home. As a child, I thought they were the originals. I had wondered how my mother, born in Juneau, Alaska, became fascinated by those Parisian scenes. They say children subconsciously fulfill their parents' unrealized dreams. Was I about to experience the life my mother hoped to live? Could that be why I felt unnaturally plunged into a world that I had never thought about before? I had never suspected my mother had dreams, let alone considered them.

To me, Utrillo painted a fantasy version of Paris covered in a scrim of mythical, insistent rain. Like Seattle. As a child, I never thought to visit it. Especially with an unpleasant Frenchman, reading the menu as if it were a vintage edition of Playboy.

Still, I felt the charm of Paris getting under my skin, despite the company. Seattle was immature, like a juvenile delinquent I knew too well. Here, local high-spirited artists roamed the narrow streets asking audaciously, *"S'il vous plaît, mademoiselle,* may I paint your portrait, *ce soir?"* offering to show me his sketches. The streets buzzed, like a hive of reckless potential.

"This is the *absolument* epitome of an authentic restaurant in Paris!" cried Michel.

I almost rolled my eyes as I sipped something sweet, scarlet, and bubbly and wanted more of that tingle. He then ordered an array of specialties the café was famous for. He was certain I'd never tasted anything like them. It was the most unappetizing assortment of items I could imagine touching my lips! Frogs' legs (the freshest in Paris), snails cooked in butter and wine, and mussels in some kind of cream sauce. At that time, I was not a vegetarian. But I drew the line at swamp creatures.

As soon as each dish appeared, he inhaled it! I wondered when he had eaten last. Or was this how the French enjoyed a meal?

"Are you sure you won't taste this last one?" He dangled a poor little leg near my mouth. "You're in a country famous in the world for its cuisine!" He winked at me, juices dripping down the corners of his mouth, as his lizard-like tongue made them disappear.

He tore off a chunk of bread and let the juices of the frog dish saturate it. I took a small crust of the baguette and tried the tasty sauce, but it did not appeal to me. I felt trapped and as if things could not get worse. How did I get into this situation? I couldn't remember the specifics, but there was a painful similarity to something from my past that he was reminding me of.

As we came to the end of this macabre meal, I thanked him for showing me this "iconic" place. (At this point I didn't wish to burn the bridge till I got safely to my hotel room.)

Finally, we headed to the center of the Left Bank, an area called Odéon. Now, at 10:30 in the evening, unfashionably late to be checking in, I happily accepted the key from the skeptical desk clerk, as Michel quickly swaggered upstairs carrying my heaviest luggage.

"I will show you a more efficient way of packing your suitcase!"

I agreed I could use some tips, but not now, God forbid.

In my room the welcoming bed beckoned me and I couldn't wait to flop into it.

"Au revoir, Michel, I'll see you tomorrow."

Michel insisted, "At this time, it is much too late for me to go home and possibly awaken my family!" He wanted to reorganize my suitcases and then share the bed, promising to remain on his side.

Exhausted, I relented, and immediately he made a pass.

"What do you think you're doing? Leave!" I yelled like a mother scolding a maddening child.

Scorned and sullen, he offered to sleep in the large chair. He won the prize for the most persistent, perverse scoundrel I'd ever encountered.

Although he'd met me with my boyfriend in the Caribbean, apparently he figured now that I was alone, I was up for grabs—and he was going to grab me!

In my life at that time, I was just beginning to reject the concept that men's desires were legitimate and mine were pointless, and I hadn't quite admitted to myself that his behavior was unacceptable and rude. I felt lousy.

It dawned on me that Michel had been wearing me down all night so that he could eventually sleep with me! Sadly, I would experience similar techniques of seduction with other unwanted European admirers. Now I was beginning to learn how to nip it in the bud. It was in Paris where I had to quickly develop personal boundaries regarding men.

Not wanting to hurt his pride or lose his favor, I said, "I guess you can sleep in the chair. Will you need a blanket?" But my brain was screaming, "Julie, you've got to *get rid of him,* not tuck him in."

"No, I'll be okay!" he pouted. He wrapped his sport coat backward around himself, like a straitjacket, and pretended to shiver. Thankfully, after a few awkward minutes, he stood up and said, "You know, you're really not a very polite or grateful woman!"

Would I ever get rid of this buffoon? I had an idea: "I'm calling your father to come and take you home." This must have struck a chord, for suddenly he looked thoughtful.

"He cannot be reached after nine."

Finally fed up, I gathered my wits and commanded, *"Va-t'en!* Leave now!" This was the one French phrase I remembered perfectly, one that should stop any man in his tracks from molesting you. It was a powerful imperative.

Did that *really* come out of my mouth? I was impressed with my chutzpah. And to ease the bite of it, sweetly I said, "Call me in the morning." But I hoped he wouldn't, as the door thudded behind him.

He was the only real contact I had in Paris so far. What baffled me was how to manage his inappropriate advances without putting a kibosh on our acquaintance. I had not met someone so ostensibly manipulative before, and being a foreigner, I hesitated to insult him since this might be their cultural norm.

I suspected that men were the problem. But now, I realized that it was me tolerating and allowing an odd scoundrel to walk on me. I wondered if this was my Achilles' heel! A hard life lesson I would wrestle with: how to say no.

I was concerned that Michel wouldn't "like" me. He had promised to connect me with influential people in Paris, but I couldn't imagine how. He wasn't in show business; he worked in his father's jewelry shop. If my first night in Paris had given me any indication of his style, I would prefer to muddle through on my own!

He called the next day wanting to show me the best way to shop. It's impossible for a girl to refuse such an opportunity, being new in Paris and not knowing where the fashionable places are. If this was to be only a month in Paris, then I wanted to be accompanied on a shopping spree by a French speaker. Little did I realize the shops were plentiful in Paris.

Greeting me with those obligatory friendly kisses again, he remarked that I didn't look as vibrant as one should look, visiting the chic boutiques. If that wasn't enough to turn me off completely, he added that I should pick up my pace, as my languorous style wasn't going to work well on these busy boulevards. I couldn't tell if he was insulting me or being helpful. There was so much to see that I had to adjust my senses to the abundance of stylish shops and well-dressed people scurrying about. I felt I couldn't do anything right. I hoped this was not a sample of French hospitality. A month here might be too long.

He took me to the most expensive shops. It was nice to look around, but I was not exactly on a quick buying holiday; I was on a budget. My luggage was bursting already. I wasn't about to add more weight to my dangerously heavy suitcases.

Michel showed me a pair of exceptionally soft calfskin gloves, pressing them to his face, saying, "These would make a beautiful gift, perhaps for you to give to someone?"

I pondered, *Yeah, maybe Tor would like these.* But I had never seen Tor wear nice gloves. He was a fisherman, not a dandy.

Then he came right out and said, "You might consider getting them for me as a gift after all I've done for you!"

I laughed, thinking he was finally being ironic, and replied, "Let me think about it . . ."

That was the last time I saw him. Later that day I called Mia Newman, my friend's sister. She was thrilled to hear from me. We made plans to meet on the weekend.

4. I Love Paris in the Fall

. . . .

The most seductive thing about art is the personality of the artist himself. — Paul Cézanne

WITH REGARD TO MONEY, TOR, a successful fisherman, generously made sure I wouldn't have to stress out that first month. Besides my small personal savings, he purchased back the car he had given me, a sassy Karmann Ghia, so I'd have a hardy supply of traveler's checks, just in case. He cautiously gave me his American Express card for emergencies. That was a scary thought. What kind of emergency was he referring to?

I'm glad he encouraged me to study French while in Paris, as I might not have thought of that. Why should I have to learn French? I didn't think I'd be there more than a month, possibly two. Still, it made perfect sense. I always took Tor's suggestions, as he seemed more logical and intelligent than I. He inspired more than one life-changing experience for me. Finding singing engagements might be a challenge, but it would be easier with some French under my belt.

In Seattle, I had taken a quick French course for travelers where a fellow classmate gushed about maybe going to Paris someday, to visit her sister currently attending the Sorbonne. I jumped on that hot tip, letting her know I would be in Paris in one month, and could I please have her sister's address so I could write to her and let her know my time frame. Maybe we could meet.

My friend replied, "Mia is studying dance and art at the Sorbonne. She's so homesick and would love to see someone from Seattle!"

Immediately, I wrote to Mia from Seattle, letting her know when I would be in Paris. She responded that she'd look forward to meeting me, giving me her phone number and address.

After my horrendous experience with Michel, my first impression upon hearing her voice on the phone was of childlike, bubbly enthusiasm. She invited me to come to her apartment, setting my mind at ease.

"Bring all your luggage, take a taxi to my place, and spend a few nights on my couch if you like. I'd love to help you find a homey hotel in my neighborhood near the Sacré-Coeur. It's a fantastic arrondissement."

"That would be wonderful," I replied, relieved to meet someone from Seattle. (Seattleites were a friendly bunch.)

Mia's apartment was five floors up, with no lift. Even though she was wearing high-heeled, laced-up-the-calf black suede boots (every fashionable female in Paris wore them), she insisted on helping me with my dangerously heavy suitcases. For a brief moment, I wished Michel might appear, but he was out of the picture. As she heaved the suitcase one stair at a time, her heel slipped on the slick cement from the girth of my baggage, and she injured her ankle. She screamed and began to cry. I was shocked and sure the whole building could hear her shriek, "I'll never dance again!"

An elderly man ventured from his apartment cautiously to see about the clatter. She assured the nosy neighbor, between sniffles, that she was OK, but *"Jamais danser encore!"* (She would never dance again.)

I was impressed with her command of French in this extreme moment. Gesturing toward my suitcase, he flapped his lips to make a motorboat sound, as if to say no one should lift such a behemoth anywhere. After resting a moment, we finally made it to the top. I followed Mia with my two smaller bags, equally heavy—she was the lead in this dance.

Once inside, she iced her ankle and told me how happy she was to meet me.

Her flat was located in the neighborhood of the Sacré-Coeur. The area was not splashy and chic, but dripping with a strange foreign quaintness, where exotic nationalities flocked to sell their baubles, camel-bone necklaces, sunglasses, and baskets to the international tourists who slowly climbed the steps up to the Basilica of the Sacré-Coeur.

Mia, with her long, dark, wild hair and carefree dancer's spirit, resembled one of Botticelli's cherubs. We were kindred souls. Like an angel, she was my helpful guide during my early days in Paris. In her sparse atelier near the Sacré-Coeur, she kept a small carton of fresh milk and peach confiture on the windowsill because, Mia insisted, "In Paris, you don't need a fridge—if you have a windowsill, why bother?" She made doing without appliances sound sublimely bohemian.

It was a basic one-bedroom apartment, and after two days of sleeping on the couch in her living room, I was ready to find my own place. It was tempting to stay, but I had come to discover a magnificent city, explore the Paris music scene, and maybe get a few gigs.

The convivial Mia loved to wander as much as I when she had free time. She guided me through the 18th arrondissement searching for just the right hotel that would be close to her place. We spied a white hotel with a wishing well conveniently located next to the Lamarck-Caulaincourt metro station that struck our curiosity. Mia did the talking, and that afternoon I moved in, not knowing how long I'd stay.

Living in the Hôtel Caulaincourt, near the foot of the Sacré-Coeur, felt secure and not intimidating. It would be a good place to plant myself for a while.

The French staff at the hotel were standoffish at first, but once they sized me up and figured out I wasn't a *crazy foreigner woman* looking for French adventures, they were helpful and liked me.

A delightful idiosyncrasy of French hotels was providing a comforting petit dejeuner every morning. They graciously brought it to my room early, if I requested it the night before—*café au lait* or *chocolat chaud* (hot chocolate) and a basket of heavenly, freshly baked croissants with several little pots of jam. I thoroughly enjoyed those breakfasts! Is there anything better to wake up to? Just enough jam and butter on warm croissants to satiate me till I could round up a lunch snack in the afternoon. The French have definitely mastered the art of hospitality.

My first few weeks in the City of Light were like learning how to do a slow dance with a new love, an extraordinary invitation to the party I always wanted to go to but never knew existed. So I respectfully made my way, like the French do, with gentility. I Immediately signed up for French classes at the Alliance Française and found it surprisingly easy to make friends with my foreign classmates. After French lessons, we'd visit landmarks like Notre-Dame, the Jardin du Luxembourg, or the iconic Shakespeare and Company bookstore, with its historic upstairs living quarters for itinerant writers.

At times we'd venture to a famous outdoor café. Café de Flore was one of my favorites, appealing to forward-thinking intelligentsia—*comme nous* (like us). Here I smoked my first Gitanes cigarette; I coughed and chatted while writing in my journal, sipping espresso with brown crystalized sugar lumps or a glass of young Beaujolais. We'd mingle with anyone in earshot. Conversing with ease about why we were in Paris, our search for jobs or apartments, or tips on adjusting to living in a vibrant city, everyone had a drama or a dream to try on for size. I would chat with anybody willing to listen, and it felt good to know I wasn't the only one stumbling around Paris, trying to get my bearings. It amused me that there were others like myself, trying to find something we couldn't find where we had come from. But why Paris? We were all youngish—twenties and thirties—crazy with brilliant ideas and wanting our careers to take shape and then flight. Times like these in Paris made one feel connected to some ethereal treasure hunt. Life felt like a party, perhaps because it was always happy hour in the cafés.

A sense of fashion was fastidiously imparted through osmosis and an occasional disapproving look if I overestimated the acceptance of my casual street attire. I guess it was the elite chic who dictated the fashion standards expected of everyone on the street, including transient internationals like *moi*. Of course, it depended on the neighborhood and on the time of day or night one happened to be gallivanting through the streets of Paris, but in general you better have cultivated a sense of style. Or be prepared to endure the Parisians' disapproving stares at your athletic shoes and parka.

The French are naturally stylish. Even the neighborhood *clochard* (the French word for a hobo) had fashion flair and knew exactly at what chic angle to drape a moth-eaten scarf dramatically around his neck, landing with just the right amount of panache, off the shoulder of his grungy overcoat while imploring passersby, *"Dix francs, s'il vous plaît?"* with a charming, semi-toothless smile, tipping his sullied hat. Since I saw him regularly in the same area, we began to greet each other, and I practiced my French on him with great buoyancy. I enjoyed the warm smile that donating a few francs earned me.

In Paris, fashion is prioritized. One stylish mademoiselle, whose main form of transportation was roller skates, confided she'd go without food rather than pass up the latest trendy fashions displayed on the humongous billboards in Saint-Germain-des-Prés.

Simply from hanging out with the exquisite Mia, in this style-conscious city, I felt an urgency to upgrade my wardrobe. Mia modeled part-time for art students at the Sorbonne. As we strolled through the Latin Quarter, a supersized billboard informed us that polka dots were the rage. At Mia's suggestion, we entered a small boutique, where I discovered an adorable pair of polka-dot slingback pumps the likes of which I'd never seen, and impulsively purchased them. Mia fortified my purchase with "In Paris, it's easy to be chic if one knows how to accessorize." I rationalized this purchase for my soon-to-be upcoming singing engagements. I wanted to cultivate the allure and mystery of the 1940s film noir vibe, originating in Paris.

On another day of wandering about with Mia, I spotted a smart chapeau with a sheer black lace veil in the window at Galeries Lafayette, the high-end department store of Paris. Capturing my imagination, though beyond my budget, the hat was mine immediately, before I could talk myself out of this splurge. Mia reminded me, "Julie, the hat was made for you! Your essence travels to another level of mystery with such a chapeau. Did you know you're one of the most beautiful women in the world? Get that hat." (Though I seldom saw anyone in Paris wearing a hat, she was so persuasive.) I knew I wanted to exude the self-assurance and élan to wear it in performances and photo shoots, and in that moment Mia pushed me over that edge.

She continued, "You're tall and curvy, with an unbelievable personality and a million-dollar smile. I've seen women here in Paris and it isn't often I see one who stands out like you!"

I was stunned to hear this, as most of my life I'd felt less than attractive. But Mia was a complex artist who saw deeply into those she observed and cared about. It was enlightening information to receive during this vulnerable time. I was a late bloomer and just entering my "sensual phase" of womanhood. It was not flattery, she insisted, touching my arm for emphasis. She may have sensed that I felt below par coming from a male-dominated Sicilian family where keeping a girl down was built into the menfolk's DNA. All in good fun too—everyone in our family laughed about it. Nothing about women was sacred. Not even the only daughter among three brothers.

Luckily, I also carried Norwegian genes on my mother's side, a matriarchal force that had begun to inspire me, as an adult, to stand up to oppression like the Viking goddesses I descended from. With Mia's affirmations and a few important accessories, I might fit into Paris just fine.

· · · · · · · · · · · · · · · · ·

On my own, without demands, I floated in musings through the districts of Paris, fading in and out of a trance. When did not knowing where I was going ever feel better? I wandered through secluded, crooked, cobblestone streets that led me to glimmering places holding ancient history. One day, stopping to rest, I entered a combination bar/café where it seemed everyone knew each other. Tentatively hoping to not be noticed I ordered *"Un croque monsieur, monsieur."* (Did that sound insipid? I wondered.) After a tasty snack, my courage restored, I paid my simple *l'addition* (bill) and counted the change I received. I was getting the hang of the French francs.

It seemed possible to never stop walking. I lost track of time and sometimes forgot to eat. Occasionally a nagging thought visited, revisited, and disappeared for no reason: *Why was I here on my own?* I wasn't sure of my ability to do this, whatever "this" was. Something was supposed to happen, and I wasn't sure what.

I continued rambling, secretly enjoying not having a schedule, like a temp job or someplace I had to be on time. I let the fragrant bouquets from the prolific flower stalls at random locations seduce my senses. When I tired of being outdoors, I stopped in boutiques, where sometimes I was the only customer and made friendly small talk with the sales clerks, practicing my French. Occasionally I felt compelled to make a purchase I didn't need, because they had been so kind to me, forgetting my bulging suitcases that weren't losing any weight. It was OK to not accomplish more than looking around; I was a foreigner, a traveler. I had to allow myself to get used to this new identity. I absorbed the unfamiliar feelings and lifestyle in never-before-seen neighborhoods and historical sites and began to allow myself to relax into "feeling French." This prepared me for the next thing lurking around each corner for this broad, abroad.

One never goes hungry for long in Paris because food is everywhere, subliminally crying out, "Don't forget to eat!" The charcuteries would have inspired my father, with his passion and acuity for sausage making and cured meats. I wished he could have seen how they did it in France. I had a special appreciation for how aesthetically they were displayed in Paris: a mouthwatering, eye-catching assortment. Sausages made from a variety of meats, delectably tender Parma ham, carpaccio, pancetta, smoked salmon and celery rémoulade. Anything you'd want for a party, a picnic, or standing at a counter for a quick snack.

The open-air farmers' fruit and vegetable markets were a theatrical experience impossible to prepare oneself for. The outspoken vendors intimidated me. It was as if I suddenly found myself an actor in a play I had not auditioned for—street theater at its finest. With penetrating voices, they demanded I speak French. When I lost my courage, they thought I was crazy. I didn't know how to say the correct words for exactly what I wanted, like how to purchase "un kilo," and sometimes I'd end up with four whole pounds of apricots, just so I could hurry away. The fruit vendors had no time to suffer fools: "Say what you want, pay for it, and be on your way!"

Sometimes they raised their voices, indignantly swearing, but since I didn't know exactly what they meant, I thought I'd kill them with kindness, and replied: *"Merci monsieur, vous êtes si gentil"* (Thanks, mister, you're so kind)—an expression I heard French people say to each other often.

It was a lucky accident to run into an open-air market, as they appeared on random mornings and afternoons in various neighborhoods.

A prolific number of appetizing boulangeries filled with beautiful, decadent pastries and breads that resembled works of art left me awestruck. They were almost too beautiful to eat. They tasted rich and more decadent than anything I was used to. I wondered how a city could have so many bakeries everywhere, yet no one seemed overweight.

I took notice of an unusually large shop, painted completely white, inside and out. One day I had the courage to go in and look around. It felt immaculately sterile and sold only cheese. It felt alive with so many "living" cheese cultures. The varieties that existed were perplexing. The smell of the store was strong and slightly nauseating to my unsophisticated nose.

"How do you tell the difference, when everything looks like some form of cream cheese?" I accidentally asked the gruff, swarthy clerk in English.

He replied in broken English, "Zee way you tell with anything you want to eat. You taste it with your mouth. *Tiens"* (Take some). He winked.

He handed me a creamy, aromatic dollop of sheep cheese on a small piece of paper and paused for my reaction. It was a gooey, strong, tangy-tasting blob. I tried to not show how uncomfortable it made me to swallow it.

"Très fort, monsieur" (Very strong, sir), I said with a sickly smile. I thought I'd better buy some or he'd get mad. I ended up with a pound and

a half of some kind of cheese, which I was still unable to eat, though I tried. I picked up a baguette and gave it to the surprised hotel staff.

When I was especially hungry, an overflowing falafel sandwich was my choice—a complete delicious meal with eggplant, olives, purple cabbage, pickled baby turnips, and tahini sauce. A handsome Egyptian fellow at his kiosk remembered me and made it just the way I liked it.

Romance was in the air, possibly in the water, and literally on the streets of Paris. A sidewalk café easily became an improvised backdrop where lovers kissed, oblivious that strangers witnessed the not-so-innocent titillations. If a photographer was in the right place at the right time, a candid shot could eventually turn into art or be in one of the many fashion magazines.

5. Père-Lachaise

"I have sometimes been wildly, despairingly, acutely miserable . . . but through it all I still know quite certainly that just to be alive is a grand thing." — Agatha Christie

PARIS WAS WAITING FOR ME! It was no accident that I'd been "summoned" by an unknown vibration, almost a kind of spooky nudge. Coming into a foreign country and attempting something seriously difficult and artistic—to be a singer and entertainer—was unlike anything I had ever considered.

When I first arrived in Paris, I felt embarrassingly conspicuous, on the loose and out of my depth. France was my first transcontinental journey and I was alone. It was obvious I was a foreigner, taller and larger than the people surrounding me. I am noticeable, even in my own country; this had been pointed out more than once, and I'd gotten used to it.

Having been in Paris only days, I began to understand the paradox that traveling alone has drawbacks and lots of benefits. On this particular day I chose to visit a famous cemetery, Père-Lachaise. Going alone to a cemetery sounds like a normal thing to do when attending a funeral of a dearly beloved someone. But, in a foreign country, where they have a multitude of great and famous poets, writers, actors, musicians, singers, rock stars, and ancient warriors and statesmen buried, there is an otherworldly, disquieting energy circulating. And Père-Lachaise is as large as six football fields! This could be daunting.

It was the chance meeting of people like Mia who helped me on the journey of improving my self-concept, of believing in the power of being who I was destined to be. Being alone in a new location, I collected encouragement from others and used their belief in me as a bridge to begin believing in my talent as a singer and to see where it might take me. Luckily, growing up I had an influential older brother, with a sardonic sense of humor, devoted to classical piano and organ. He helped develop and influence my style. He was instrumental in helping me develop my sense of humor and musicality. I believed if I had those two things going for me, everything would be OK.

It was a powerful tonic to travel and free-fall into a new world, and see what it would take to adapt, to reach, and to become more than I thought I could be. Paris as a threshold appeared to guide my stepping into the world differently. Something I hadn't imagined before.

I swerved fearfully at first into this new realm of "abroad-ness." This was the enchanting, unreal, aesthetic universe of Paris 1983. I was emboldened with lists of places to visit and friends of friends to call on. I didn't do much research beforehand to understand the immensity of what I was taking on; I was afraid it might scare me out of going.

I planned to check out the sights as soon as possible to understand how the city worked, the way you want to hurry to know the details about a new friend. I heard the best way to know a city was to fall in love. I wanted to intimately know Paris, but deep affection takes time, preparation, effort, and, most importantly, providence.

The dilemma for me was going everywhere alone at first. I hated all those learning curves, yet that's what eventually made my time there more meaningful. I became skilled at navigating one of the most spectacular cities of the world.

My first days in Paris—alone—gave me the opportunity to own my personal impression, without anyone influencing my perceptions. As much as I longed for someone, if I had had a friend to chat with, I might have been distracted from what I was meant to experience.

As a woman traveling solo in Paris, one is never long without a man if you want one. (I've always wanted one!) The French are hopeless romantics, which gave me, after living in Seattle all my life, a feeling of *Finally, a city that gets it*. The French never give up the hope of experiencing love in a *coup de foudre*—a bolt of lightning or love at first sight. Paris was built for romance. Whether or not they were *in love*, everyone in Paris looked like they were just coming or going from a tryst, or heartbroken from a lost love, or hurrying home with lots of delicious food from the market to cook for the one they love, or, my favorite to observe, lovers holding hands and kissing passionately along the Seine. At least, that's the story I told myself until I got to know the stark reality of many affairs.

I felt comfortable in Paris, more so than anywhere. There was an air of gentility and charm oozing out of every neighborhood, and I felt unbridled astonishment crossing every ornate bridge. I was fearless in crowded streets—no matter what time of night. A few cryptic comments were made by a certain kind of man, which I didn't understand. I internalized the mantra "Ignorance is bliss!"

Getting around was easy with the efficient metro (subway), a plethora of easy-to-find taxis, and walking. You didn't need a car unless you went outside Paris.

That early morning in October, I got on the right metro and knew the stop: Père-Lachaise. I gravitated to this eclectic, ancient cemetery where various luminaries were buried, like Edith Piaf, Jim Morrison, Gertrude Stein, Alice B. Toklas, Oscar Wilde, Sarah Bernhardt, Chopin, and Maria Callas, to name a few I wished to pay my respects to.

Perhaps my decision to visit Père-Lachaise signified the end of something I had been living in Seattle—relinquishing the status quo of being a sought-after comedic singer and a big fish in a small pond. I left behind the relationship questions (like, *Was he "right" for me?*) and the frustration of trying to discover myself while living in a traditional box, fitting into some kind of mold, when my wild soul yearned for Bohemia and the bright lights.

I secretly felt the desire to succeed, but on some level I knew that in order to bloom, I might have to go *elsewhere*, far from everything and everyone familiar. I needed to put the past aside—perhaps even bury it—

and rise as a phoenix into a more dynamic direction.

The cemetery of Père-Lachaise is where I'd chosen to stretch my parameters. Nervously I reread the directions: *Take the metro to the end of the line. The name of the stop is Père-Lachaise.* This sounded too easy, which made me worry.

It was a foggy morning, gray and cold. At 9:00 a.m. I observed workers getting on and then exiting the train at different stops. They didn't look particularly chic. Abruptly the train was almost empty. Yet there were many stops listed on the upper informational panels before the end of the line, *Cimetière du Père-Lachaise*.

I was edgy about missing my stop, but since it was the last, I figured I'd have time to ask a conductor, if there would still be one on the train. I was trying to feel happy about visiting Edith Piaf's grave. I hoped her spirit would inspire my audacity.

There's nothing like a solo outing to a cemetery on a somber, dreary morn. I wondered if this was a wise choice. Though I was on the precipice of discovering something, I felt homesick and sad during those first days of exploration in Paris, having left my cozy, taken-care-of state of existence in Seattle and my precious dog, Sophie. She would have happily joined me in the necropolis and I wouldn't have felt frightened and lonely. The guidebook had warned me it was best to get there before the throngs arrived, and as far as cemeteries go, that it was definitely a sight to see! (I tried to stoke the embers of my diminishing courage to explore everything in Paris.)

The train had cleared out—like a ghost train!—except for that one average-looking guy sitting a few seats in front of me, approximately my age.

I was now wound up and palpitating with fear. I tried to size him up, as if he were the last man on earth. I guessed he wasn't French. He could have been anything. In fact, he looked American, all bundled up in a parka, stoic and not flirtatious.

I spoke first. Being an entertainer had given me a reckless decorum to instigate conversations with complete strangers. In fact, I'm better at that than talking to people I know. I said in French, *"Excusez moi, vous-connaissez Père-Lachaise?"*

Smiling, he said, "I'm going there too. I'm American."

A joyous discovery for us! We were both from the States and going to the same place, a grateful coincidence for me. We became instant companions. He was from Baltimore, a basic nice guy who'd been traveling throughout Europe for a couple of months. And after visiting Père-Lachaise, he would be on his way back to the States. In fact, he was departing the very next day.

It was ideal to connect with a clean-cut, attractive, no-agenda single man.

We shared the reasons we happened to be in Paris: me to sing, he—at the end of his travels through Europe—to see a few sights before he returned to the States to start his new job. We talked easily to each other as if we were matching spirits. We were both at turning points in our lives as we converged at this unique destination.

He was optimistic about my success in Paris—he said he could feel it would happen. I treasured hearing that. In my solitude during those first weeks, living in a hotel, I was easily losing my certainty of continuing on my own in this unpredictable lifestyle. But he was one of the angels I met on my date with destiny in Paris.

Oscar Wilde's gravesite was at the top of our mutual lists to visit—especially for me since he, too, came from a background of theater and poetry. We discovered the difficult-to-find grave of Jim Morrison as well. I was glad I had found a friend to accompany me in this foreboding, ominous graveyard. He, unlike me, could read a map. One could sense—in the ancient, ruined places where the mysterious veil between life and death felt thin—vibrations of spirits and heavy-hearted, lost souls that were lingering in this peculiar miasma. Trees were not vibrant and green but drooping canopies; weeping willows, not quite dead, not alive, languished in a sort of netherworld. The once lush, life-filled flowers had been left neglected since the summer. A heaviness hung in the air, and I wasn't sure I wanted to stay too long. Although it was daylight, the ornately carved sculptures and sepulchers, crypts, and mausoleums were dark and eerie once inside the gates. An occasional lit candle would flicker, and I wondered who lit this candle so early in the morning. There were crumbling gravestones dated from the 1700s and dedications in French. I came to the conclusion that there was a mysterious sadness and loveliness about the end of life, including enchantment and madness hiding in the midst. I felt a lonely desolation walking around this ancient, ageless place.

Kneeling at Edith Piaf's gravesite, where a candle burns eternally, I said a prayer imploring her spirit to befriend me in Paris as I hoped to make my way as a singer and find similar opportunities and happiness. There were signs that less-than-respectful onlookers had visited her burial ground: cigarette butts, an empty wine bottle, and wrappers from cheap snacks. There were fresh flowers around the mausoleum, and I felt sorry that I hadn't thought to bring a token or gift. I guess my visit was a sort of gift. While studying her name and the meticulous care and beauty of her gravestone, I felt a ghostly chill and macabre vibrations bubbling up. I was ready to move on sooner than I imagined I would.

The cemetery is huge and I was ready for a break from the morbid atmosphere.

He suggested, "Let's visit a café for *chocolat chaud* to warm up." We crossed the street. *Père-Lachaise was one of many destinations*, I thought to myself; I could surely return again another day, since I had a feeling I would be in Paris for a while.

6. Unhinged Canadian Singer

Not everyone will understand our journey; that's fine, it's not their journey to make sense of. — Zero Dean

IT WAS TIME TO STOP WANDERING AROUND PARIS drunk with the bombardment of beauty everywhere and begin the somewhat tawdry escapade of looking for a place to sing. Checking out the vibes of various jazz clubs and restaurant-bars, I listened to singers and tried to imagine myself in their places. I was measuring the quality that was expected in the local clubs. Some were located deep in underground caves where the quality of the air was questionable and it was refreshing to escape. Here a variety of musical talents, from drummers to horn players, singers to tap dancers, would show up and wait to do their thing. I feverishly read the listings in *Pariscope* and decided jam sessions would be a great place to meet other singers and connect with their pipeline to the action.

I stopped at a club off Place Saint-Michel on a short side street, Rue de Buci. It looked like a happening scene, packed with revelers, live musicians, and a female vocalist, singing with her heart and soul a song that stopped me in my tracks as I entered the club.

"And he pisses like I cry for an unfaithful love!" she lamented from the stage, as if spitting out the last cries of desperate living. The song was "Amsterdam," and little did I know that someday I would sing that exact lyric while on a cruise ship entering the actual port of Amsterdam.

When I first heard that infamous line, it exploded into my every brain cell, melted into my solar plexus, and bounced up to take residence in my heart. I had to have that song!

It was written and first recorded by Jacques Brel, the Belgian-born singer-songwriter renowned in France and throughout Europe for his storylike poignant songs of passionate desperation. It was a lyric unlike any kind I'd ever heard, and I deeply connected to it. I wished I'd written that line!

During the singer's rendition of the tune, I was riveted. When she finished, I was altered, stunned. Something really important had just happened to me, but I wasn't sure what it was. It was one of those intense moments when a song demands that you sing it! In other words, an invitation by the muse.

Not wanting to let it get away or become impossible to find (which can happen with a song), I was like a hound on a scent. I loved having discovered this European genre of dramatic song! I introduced myself to the singer, thinking she might like to be my friend. I was having pretty good luck in that department in Paris. I was the new girl in town, exuding carefree self-reliance and tonight sporting a newly purchased pair of outrageously long, dangling coral earrings. Plus, as usual when I meet new people, I was bubbling over with my cool, raw charisma and enthusiasm. It was so easy to pretend I was somebody extraordinary back then.

"That was great," I told her. "You had an amazing delivery of that song." She smiled at the comment, as she made small talk in English with other members of the audience. "What was the name of that song you sang?" I asked nonchalantly, trying not to sound too insanely interested.

"'Amsterdam,' ya know, from the musical *Jacques Brel Is Alive and Well and Living in Paris*? I did the show in Calgary last year."

She appeared to be in charge of the jam session, but soon I realized she was just another controlling singer, emerging from the group of other singers eagerly waiting to perform, each hoping this would become their next gig.

I told her I was from Seattle and looking for gigs in Paris. She responded with an edge, "There are no gigs in Paris! I've been here three months. I'm going back to Canada next week."

Since it was a jam session, I asked her where to sign up. She muttered, "At the foot of the stage."

It was the first time I'd been to this hidden bar in the Latin Quarter, where you wouldn't expect to find a country-and-western joint with the name Montana's. The French weren't ready then—nor will they ever be—for a country-and-western bar! I heard that overnight it had transformed into a hot jazz club, and that turned the tide. However, the saddle on the bar and photos of famous cowboys, like the Lone Ranger and Billy the Kid, were reminders of the bar's former incarnation.

Jazz had made Montana's a happening! And the proof was the small but loyal crowd of French beatnik types and hopeful singers in the audience, along with a few throwbacks wearing pointed cowboy boots, smoking Marlboros, and drinking straight whiskey.

The lights in clubs were always kept low in Paris at night; what more could you desire? The pianist was a vintage French hippie with a bassist and drummer. They seemed joyfully engaged at having a happening jazz gig accompanying an array of singers.

A disembodied voice announced my name from the dark room. My turn to sing my song; I chose "La Vie en Rose." I checked in with the musicians and gave them my music, describing the tempo by singing a tiny bit of it to them.

"I'll sing the introductory verse rubato, so follow me." I checked the eyes of the pianist to see if he was tracking my instructions. "Then, go into the song as a medium bossa nova ballad." I smiled, assuming someone in the trio understood English. We got underway and I milked the French lyrics, recalling the first time I sang "La Vie en Rose" to a French audience on the island of Saint Martin. The audience stopped talking. As I got into the heart of the song, I took a risk and "worked the crowd," pretending they were my long-lost friends from another planet. In Seattle, I'd been rewarded with this method of creating connection. In theater parlance, it's called "breaking the fourth wall." I gave the best rendition I could manage without a rehearsal, and with a band that had possibly played the song too many times with too many singers!

I finished with an emotional vamping of the ending, repeating the catchphrase "La vie en rose, la vie en rose." Not a soul in the place looked familiar, but the natives seemed friendly. I had only sung in French a few times in my career. This song meant something to me that my heart had wrestled with since I was a child, but I still wasn't sure what that was. They applauded, and I wondered if it was for my interpretation or for the mysterious emotion that human beings feel and are confused by most of their lives. Anemoia.

While the applause trailed off, I headed to the bar for my reward. The bartender smiled knowingly, handing me a Kir royal with a pink straw. The free drink offered to the singers.

The Canadian siren approached me cautiously through the maze of tables, chairs, and drunks, then lunged like a predatory leopard. I'd imagined she wanted to compliment me, but as she came into focus, her rapid approach seemed more like she might bite! She blasted off a litany of performance notes, a "full frontal attack"!

"You should never interact with French people while you're singing, they don't like that!" *(How would she know?)* "Your pronunciation is terrible! It's insulting to the French to try to speak French when you're so bad at it!" *(At least I tried.)* "Your earrings are too long, and your face is long, it makes your face look longer!"

That was the first time I'd ever been told I had a long face, but it wouldn't be the last. And this offensive woman wasn't done yet. The singer bellowed with barely concealed venom in her eyes—or was that simply a case of day-old eye makeup?—"The dress you're wearing is too short and you need to change that song . . ."

I froze. Did confrontations like this actually happen between strangers? Even in a bar? None that I had ever seen. (And I've darkened the door of quite a few dives in my day.)

"I'm telling you these things to help you have a smooth time in Paris," she continued. "I'm going back to Canada in a few days. I've been here three months without booking a single gig. Plus, it's practically impossible to get a *carte d'identité*."

I didn't have one, just my passport, which I carried at all times. Americans were able to stay in France for only three months. After that they could leave the country or visit London to get their passport restamped. Then they were free to return for three more months. It was a genteel way to keep things uncomplicated, and these requirements were often generously overlooked by the French as they loved having American jazz musicians cycle through their numerous clubs. I understood that most expat musicians, unless they were legitimately employed in the system, were paid under the table.

I thought, *Good to know you're leaving!*

Then she warned, "I'd like to stay, but there are no gigs here."

Again, silently I thought, *For you, maybe.*

"You really nailed that song!" I gushed. I had fallen in love with "Amsterdam," and she had sung it with unselfconscious conviction.

I pretended that everything she said was helpful and that I appreciated it. On the inside, though, I was reeling from the sting of her harsh critique. I wasn't sure what to do, or how long I could stay in her proximity without a little retaliation. I remained neutral, yet ready for action. Was it foolish of me to just stand there and take her tirade? I let her go on with it, sure she was having a meltdown. I was trying to be the bigger person, rationalizing that *she just didn't get me.*

I felt a twisted compassion for her bitterness in having to say goodbye to Paris. But I was grateful that it would make more room for *me*!

A singer opens her heart when she performs, and when she returns to earth from the stage, she's still raw, maybe even bleeding. A stranger had never spoken to me like that! Was this how Canadians behaved? Maybe she was trying to pick a catfight with her American competition? I wasn't sure.

I am not good with criticism, and no one outside my family ever talked to me so callously. I hadn't learned yet that I didn't actually have to take abuse. I considered leaving, but I didn't want to back down. I appeared tough, even strong; I stood there. But I really didn't know what to do with all the negativity she emanated.

She was a real Gorgon. This was the most awkward behavior I'd faced since my traumatic run-in at Charles de Gaulle with Michel on my first night in Paris. I needed to cultivate some reinforcements and know when to bring them on. I *knew* how to fight back and cut to the quick. I grew up with three hard-hitting brothers, an outspoken Sicilian father, and a mother who was half Norwegian and half barracuda! But I didn't want that history to color my interactions.

I was playing for higher stakes than a hair-pulling contest in a makeshift Parisian jazz club with an identity crisis. She was an unhinged loser from Calgary, who'd thankfully soon return to where she came from. She had little to offer anyone—except perhaps me. *I wanted that song!*

I sweetly thanked her for the suggestions and said, "I'll try to work on all that. Oh, by the way, do you have a copy of 'Amsterdam'? You sing it so well."

"Here, have this copy," she replied, handing me the music. "I've got the score back in Canada."

I was amazed I had the guts to ask for what I wanted and that she had handed it over so readily. Had it been me, I don't know if I would have been so generous. I felt a twinge of guilt.

Fabulous songs that you can really sink your teeth into are gold and should be guarded, or else another singer might start to sing them and dilute the novelty for your audience. It's a form of creating and controlling a certain mystique to sing songs that are really yours! Songs that speak to your soul do not come along every day. I am not sure why a song as obscure as "Amsterdam" resonated so deeply with me, but why question it. I didn't know of anyone singing it at the time, and over the years I got a lot of mileage out of it both in Europe and in the States.

There are certain boundaries in all disciplines that keep one's art pure. Still, her giving me that chart was an expression of generosity. I don't give my favorite songs away until I've recorded them or am ready to relinquish them. I am referring mainly to obscure, difficult-to-find, unpublished songs, which I've had professionally transcribed from recordings for me.

Luckily, that singer didn't last long in Paris. Symbolically, by giving me the music for "Amsterdam," she handed me the torch to sing it there. She was on her way out: broke, angry, and envious. Her time was up. She would soon disappear into the ethers of faraway Canada. Mean girls never last long in cool places, and you only get one chance in Paris. Despite what anyone says, Paris is a city of gentility.

I had to earn the right to sing "Amsterdam" and had to learn it quickly! I would make it mine. The muse had spoken to me again. Perhaps that was the reason I endured this woman's remarks, holding back my anger and tears, rather than reacting or walking away. "Amsterdam" became one of my showstopping hits in Paris and other places around the world.

7. The Kindness of Strangers

I've always depended on the kindness of strangers.
— Blanche DuBois in Tennessee Williams's
A Streetcar Named Desire

It was a little late in the day to have lunch, but the cafés along the small street off the Champs-Élysées were bustling. It was mid-October, a tinge of summer hanging in the air, lending warmish days before the darkness of fall and then winter.

I had just finished my beginning French class for the day at the Alliance Française. This storybook-like, elegant neighborhood in the 8th arrondissement piqued my curiosity. It was a captivating area to find myself in for a couple of hours, three days per week. Eventually I hoped to attain at least a minimal command of the French language. It was harder than Spanish, but I recalled that learning languages takes both effort and a creative proclivity for it, which I liked the sound of possibly having. I had an inherent ease with learning lyrics in French, Spanish, and Italian, although speaking them fluently was not my forte.

Besides the chic French, there were gentry of every nationality with specific reasons for being in this neighborhood—like the impressive African embassies of Malawi, Algeria, and Egypt. Major airlines I'd never heard of before were located there—Virgin Air, Lufthansa, Aeroflot, and Air Berlin—as well as designer showrooms: Chanel, Christian Dior, and Vogue.

Soldiers with loaded rifles stood at attention, aware of each passerby. A soft wind moaned through the autumn leaves, tossing them gently about the adjoining promenades, promising changes to come. Or that something memorable could happen any moment and probably would.

I'd been in Paris for two weeks. I liked this particular language school, as several of the students seemed like good contacts and potential friends—if I stayed longer than one month. There was Joe, a future dress designer from Denmark via Barbados. And Patrick, a young Irish woman working as an au pair, with a penchant for living life to the max in Paris. We were excitable, with dreams awaiting us, wanting to learn how to navigate and mine the riches and experiences that would surely be possible in Paris if we could all speak a little French.

Still on the Champs-Élysées after French class, I was hungry. I wasn't in the mood to return to my small hotel room. I hadn't yet figured out my approach for finding singing opportunities because I simply had to get my footing in this sensational international city. My feet had to get to know the streets, as well as the impossibly esoteric names of the metro stops!

I needed to strategize, but it was hard to do when I didn't know anyone. Plus, that wasn't my style. I liked taking things as they came (laissez-faire style). I would often try and then try even harder to make things happen in my career and personal life. I noticed that when I *stopped* was when I suddenly found myself in Paris.

As I contemplated my next move, I almost missed the black Rolls-Royce parked in front of the attractive bistro I was considering for lunch. The restaurant was filled with animated, stylish French people finishing up their enjoyable lunches with coffee and cigarettes. I was envious; why couldn't I do something like that? I might even take up smoking to become a little more French! The clothes I was wearing didn't measure up to how others were dressed. They were stylish, with casual elegance and sans souci! You know, carefree yet sexy and fun, not vulgar. I felt like I needed to shed these Seattle gray-blues. I had flamboyant, vintage beaded gowns and lots of drag for the stage, but the streets of Paris were another kind of stage that I had no wardrobe for. It was not a rehearsal. They weren't waiting for "someday" to start dressing with style or living their lives—they were doing it now.

The man in the Rolls must have noticed me looking at his car as he rolled down the tinted window. There was a flirtatious vibe in the Parisian air. He was darkly handsome and soigné (well groomed) as if he'd just stepped out of the barbershop. I wondered what kind of person drove such a car. His casual "Bonjour" surprised me, and I responded, "Bonjour!" hoping I sounded French.

"Etes-vous américaine?" he asked, smiling with enthusiasm. I liked his teeth.

"*Oui! Je suis américaine, et une chanteuse du jazz!*" I squinted at completing a full sentence in French as well as to see his face more clearly.

The mention of "jazz singer" was a game changer, and I made a note of it. From then on, I used it as my ace in the hole in Paris. Most French people's interest perked up when they heard the word *jazz*, remembering WWII, when Americans saved the French from the Nazis and brought, as an added bonus, the music of American liberation: jazz! There was definitely affection between the French and Americans, and I hoped to reap the benefits of that.

He told me he was originally from Persia. Where the heck was that? I wondered. I was pretty sure I knew, but it wasn't that important.

We chatted like old friends, as he was a safe distance from me in the Rolls and I was on the sidewalk. I was still wondering about my day: Should I return to my hotel, go to some museum, or take a chance and go to a restaurant alone?

"Would you like to have lunch?" He read my mind. His sonorous voice spoke an educated English; he sounded like Omar Sharif. He gestured spontaneously toward the appealing eatery. My stomach grumbled, "Feed me!" I paused for decorum but then figured it all seemed safe enough. What could happen at lunch? It's dinnertime when things get dangerous.

"*Quelle heure est-il?*" (What time is it?) I stalled.

"It's 2:30, not too late for *déjeuner*" (lunch).

Pourquoi pas? (Why not?) I thought and answered, *"Oui!"* I liked him; he was pleasant and unafraid to make a somewhat courageous move. A few moments passed, more than necessary, I thought, as he got out of the car with effort.

I noted he had a serious disability. On one of his shoes, he wore a primitive, built-up orthopedic sole, while the other shoe was normal. As a child, I had seen this kind of malady and I had a sense of the great misfortune this person must have had to endure. The fellow sensed my reaction and quickly assured me that this ailment was from a car accident, not a deformity. For some reason that was strangely reassuring to him and me too. (As if he might be the future father of my children!)

As we walked slowly, carefully into the lively luncheonette, I felt self-consciously taller than he. The restaurant went suddenly quiet as we, the aliens, entered the mysterious but inviting environment. The efficient maître-d' led the way to a shadowy booth near the back and immediately set two Kir royals before us. Deliciously intoxicating. The brasserie resumed a lively crescendo once again. I finally relaxed into the seductive comforts of landing somewhere pleasant, enveloped in the lulling shadows, with the aroma of delicious food and drink beckoning us both into an intimate conversation about who we were and hinting at who we might become.

I ordered an omelet, the only thing I recognized on the menu, as we talked about everything, in English, for what seemed a long time: my dreams and his nightmare from a childhood car accident. I jokingly told him he shouldn't have been driving at his age! He laughed, sadly, and said, *"Vous-êtes charmante"* (you're charming). I wondered if I'd made a faux pas, making light of something so obviously grave, with a man who was still an unknown. (How many more times in my life would I say something so terribly inappropriate?) He was gracious and assured me Parisians would like me very much.

Changing the subject, he said, "You would love Iran." I had no idea where that was, and at the moment I didn't care. I was in Paris and focused on discovering why!

This was the beginning of *my* fairy tale. It wasn't about the destination. It was about something larger—the seemingly small things that happened, and the people who had nothing to do with show business who intercepted my journey, reminding me to embrace it all.

Overlooking and forgetting another's physical handicap wasn't as difficult as I imagined it might be. I compassionately accepted myself more and received a heartfelt treasure valuing this providential ambassador's kindness encouraging me on my precarious path into this beautiful dream of Paris.

8. Synchronicity in the Soap Suds

What is meant for you will find you.
—Unknown

I HAD BEEN IN PARIS FOR A LITTLE OVER TWO WEEKS, living at the Hôtel Caulaincourt, at the bottom of the mystical Sacré-Coeur. This necessitated visiting the neighborhood *laverie* (laundromat). I thought it best to master this practical necessity while I had little else going on. Bracing myself for another learning curve, I started translating the French version of the American laundromat into my challenged mind.

Entering an oblong room of metallic washers and dryers, I stepped gingerly into my first laundromat in Paris. On this mellow Friday morning, I thought I was alone until I noticed an athletic young man, about my age, casually stretched out on a mundane bench behind the wall of dryers, reading. (Could he be a terrorist? They used to hang out in Paris.) He was doing his laundry too! *Quelle coincidence!*

How could a man and a woman, alone together in a French laundromat, not speak to each other? Impossible! I broke the ice by asking him in clumsy French how to use the coin machines.

"*Excusez moi monsieur, voulez vous aider moi . . . ?*"

He glanced up from his book, not smiling, but not frowning. He answered my question with his question.

"American?" He laid his book down.

"*Oui, monsieur, vous connaissez, a* coin machine? *Comment. . . ?*"

"Speak to me in English," he directed. "That I can understand."

Shrugging his shoulders toward the slack-jawed attendant asleep at his desk, the young man with the patience of a priest kindly got up and showed me how to convert French francs into laundromat tokens. Simple things with a slight twist were quite humbling.

"Welcome to Paris," he said jovially as he inserted the tokens into the machine, and as the washer began to whirl, added, "My name is Jordan."

"I'm Julie. How do you happen to speak such great English?"

"Being half American helps. My mother is French; I work as a journalist for the *International Herald Tribune*. It's a daily English-language newspaper published in Paris," he replied.

I'd never met a person named Jordan, and I liked that name.

Pro that he was, he began asking questions immediately to get my story.

"I'm a jazz singer!" I glowed and almost stopped, recalling the harsh jazz teacher from my recent past in Seattle who cautioned me: "You can't call yourself a jazz singer unless you totally understand jazz theory and every time signature you're singing in."

I learned music by ear, and it had been working for me. I ignored her warning, naively believing jazz singing was bravado, passion for a song, staying on pitch, and, most importantly, being entertaining. It bothered me that she insisted there was much to learn when all I wanted to do was sing!

"Just watch me," I had staunchly said to myself. I'd been singing since I was a kid and my musical education started in the womb with my parents' love of jazz, big bands, and all sorts of singers, from Frank Sinatra and Mario Lanza to Judy Garland and Dinah Washington.

Jordan warmed up, and now that we were on what seemed an even playing field, we bantered, going from one topic to another. I learned that this happens when you travel. I shared my recent experience of traveling on the metro to Père-Lachaise and almost dying of fright when everyone had left the train except for one stranger and me. He interrupted my riveting story with "I've got friends who are music producers! They're looking for a singer who can write English lyrics for their disco songs and record them."

"I write songs all the time," I said. Although I did it just for fun, he didn't need to know that.

All ears, I couldn't believe this pivotal conversation popped up in a laundromat! Don't you just adore laundromats?

Noticeably interested, he added, "There's a party at one of the producers' place. Can you go this Saturday night? I'll tell them about you. You could meet them in a casual atmosphere."

Jotting the address on a small piece of paper, he said, unfazed, "Show up around 8:00 p.m. It's in the 16th arrondissement, an impressive neighborhood. I'll see you there."

I accepted the offer, as I planned to do with every enticing invitation I received. I'm no fool. It sounded like a perfect opportunity to expand my musical network.

Going to an unknown place alone was not my biggest concern. It was part of the musical territory I knew: driving to gigs, finding strange addresses, performing at private parties, as well as weddings and funerals. My main concern here would be to make a great impression by being as charming as possible, and if they asked me, I would sing "I Love Paris."

. . . .

On Saturday, as I relaxed in the comfort of a taxi, it felt luxurious to be transported by a driver who knew precisely how to find the party without getting lost and to know I didn't have to perform there unless I wanted to.

Semi-crashing this party, I rang the bell with unexpected trepidation. I felt there was a good chance I might do something socially "incorrect," just being me. Not to mention those bidets! I hoped someone would eventually explain those to me.

The French welcoming *bisous* or air-kiss greetings (for both hellos and goodbyes) always threw me for a loop, as it did when I entered the party. I had no idea who the man was who answered the door, but he was friendly and kissed me. French people seemed to be affectionate with everyone. They'd kiss me, so I'd kiss them back, inadvertently leaving my mark on their cheeks—especially with CoverGirl's Fire and Ice as my signature. A female guest observing at this party said politely, with a lukewarm smile, "You don't actually kiss them! You gently brush your cheek against theirs and it looks like a kiss! Leaving lipstick is a faux pas in Paris!" Pointing to the guests in the room, she observed, "They have your red lips on their faces!" I was secretly proud—as well as mortified—and hoped I hadn't offended anyone. How come no one mentioned that to me before? Well, I hadn't been in such a large group of kissable French people before, and usually when I was with new people, they didn't seem to mind the kiss or the lipstick. I imagined they thought it was a sweet, temporary souvenir they could easily scrub off à la toilet.

While doing the hard work of getting oriented in this unbelievable wonderland of Paris, I didn't know exactly what I was doing, but I felt that soon I should chart some kind of course. During this fallow time, I anguished, "Is life passing me by? What am I doing in Paris? What should I do next?" Yet, on another level, unseen scenarios were percolating. That Saturday night, everything changed for me and I had something to live for! I had my first inspiration to dress up and pull out my reinforcements with a simple black dress and my recently purchased, extraordinary polka-dot pumps. (I soon realized that it was more beneficial to look fabulous than to be comfortable in Paris.) An auspicious vibe in the air implied things were falling into place, starting to make sense, like in a film.

My first French soiree was going to be the start of something big, like only a party in Paris could be. No one familiar, everyone stylish, warm, and interesting—an eclectic, smart group of strangers. I was the "new girl in town," and people were curious, and maybe even envious. The vibe was pleasant, considering I knew only Jordan.

The hostess, a dark-haired beauty, and her producer husband of Algerian descent welcomed me with the warmth of newfound friends. She had made a tantalizing Algerian appetizer; it was as if I'd entered another world of taste sensation. I had to ask her, "What exactly is this? It's so delicious!"

She graciously shared her recipe, as I will share with you, dear reader, since it was so spectacular. Bon appétit!

"We have it often," she said. "First, char the red peppers in the broiler. When they blister and turn black, place them in a brown paper bag for a few hours till they sweat. Remove the skins, seeds, and extra liquid. Then slice them very thin, put them in a shallow bowl with fresh mint, garlic, a delicious olive oil, and salt, and serve them."

Sometimes when I make it at home for special occasions, for a brief moment I'm transported to the sweet succulence of that jubilant evening in Paris.

Jordan, smiling, came to my side.

"Julie, I was afraid you might change your mind!" he exclaimed as he kissed me on the cheeks! (Those were real kisses!) Responding to his demonstrative warmth, his keen and curious mind, and his helpful personality, I found everything about him appealing.

I speculated, briefly, on why people in Seattle weren't more like this. Was it because the French didn't know me yet, and had high musical hopes for this wayfaring stranger? Jordan now formally introduced me to the producers and their wives.

"This is the talented American jazz singer I was telling you about," he gushed enthusiastically.

Blushing with embarrassment, I wondered how I was going to live up to his introduction. I prayed they would not ask me to sing that night.

Amiable intros to Jean Pierre, the lead producer, and the other one led us to organize a future studio date where they would present their music tracks. I could then decide if I would be inspired to write lyrics for them, which I would then sing and they would record. They didn't seem too concerned about my singing ability. Nothing entered my mind regarding possible payment, as I was flattered and shocked that they were interested in me for something that I had only dabbled in over the years. I was hoping to find musicians in Paris to collaborate with and eventually form a group. Hooking up with music producers was skipping a few steps. They gave me their telephone numbers. This was a significant turning point whether it worked out or not. I felt as though I was suddenly in demand for something that still felt tenuous to me. Perhaps working with these music producers would reveal talents that they were determined to find in me. I was someone they wanted to work with!

I resumed mingling with Jordan and hoped he'd stay by my side, until his offhand comment that his girlfriend would be showing up later. But then my mood changed from disappointment to hope when he unexpectedly presented me to his younger cousin, Jerry, who was fresh out of the army. Slightly naive, for a French man he was unnaturally tall and Rock Hudson handsome. Half Italian, half French, half man, half boy. Perfect timing for me, as I felt somewhat vulnerable and needed a bodyguard, escort, friend. In his broken English and French accent, Jerry explained how he'd completed his mandatory military duty and was now trying to get a job as a chef. He knew how to cook well and cut vegetables like a real pro. He wanted to make up for "lost time and get a job as soon as possible in a restaurant." Oh my goodness . . . why couldn't he have been a musician? Even though I was in my late twenties, I felt mature enough to be his mother.

It was tempting to conveniently forget I had someone back home waiting for me. Tor had generously instigated, encouraged, and financially supplemented this French experience, although I felt I was going out on a limb, preparing arrangements and predicaments—not to mention the angst of living in constant uncertainty. I needed friends!

I contemplated Tor, back in Seattle happily remodeling his kitchen, vicariously enjoying my exotic discovery of Paris in ways he'd never attempt. I threw myself into unknown social situations, networking constantly while looking around for singing possibilities by meeting strangers and trying to find the right set of circumstances. My radar was up for meeting "helpful others." Through letters, phone calls, and an occasional American Express bill for a wardrobe emergency, I shared my discovery of Paris with him. I enjoyed telling people I had a boyfriend, especially since he was inexplicably not "around." It kept me safe from vultures and was a good way to stay on the trajectory of finding gigs in Paris. Was this wrong? I really wasn't even sure if I knew the difference between right and wrong. I was on the front lines in survival mode, alone.

The younger cousin, Jerry, was infatuated with the idea of showing me around Paris, and proudly at that. I understood I might be considered a trophy American girlfriend! Not every French dude had one of those! He was masculine and hunky and seemed ready to have his life start up with a new girl at his side, even if only in appearance.

I'd never considered a much younger man as a friend before, unless he happened to be gay, which Jerry was not. I had typically been attracted to more esoteric, intellectual types. Jerry was the type of simple kid who might have played football in high school and that had been the apex of achievement. I wanted someone to mindlessly escort me to places that I didn't relish going to alone, particularly places outside Paris.

One of these was Versailles. After having met at the party, we made a sort of date to take the train there for a day trip, a mini adventure. As that trip and other outings unfolded, we found we were quickly becoming pals and caught up in the magic of Paris, not really knowing each other but pretending it didn't matter, because it didn't. People would stop and stare—we were like live theater on the street, and the French are suckers for public displays of romantic intrigue!

Off a ledge of a fountain, I leapt into his arms, and he twirled me about as if we were in a remake of *An American in Paris*. We performed innocent rites of love as was expected on such an outing. The crowd looked on, smiling, perhaps wondering if we were lovers.

Taking me by the hand, he showed me as much as he could of Paris: the Jardin du Luxembourg, where we shared cotton candy (*barbe à papa*, "daddy's beard") while sitting on a park bench watching a commedia dell'arte puppet show (Was I really doing all this?); a boat ride on the Seine; the Eiffel Tower, the Louvre, Nutella crepes and croque monsieur at a buzzing corner café where the locals met. It was like Disneyland, with a hint of the demimonde for adults.

Intoxicated with the fantasy that everything was almost perfect, I was holding hands freely and felt happy to be doing so. I knew, however, that I had to put a stop to my easy flirtation before something more serious transpired. I liked a little romance as much as the next person, but I hoped Jerry wasn't falling hard for me, *profondément amoureux*.

At times I asked myself, *Am I using my time wisely, being shown Paris? Don't I need to make a splash in the Paris music scene and get my career off the ground?*

I missed Tor. He had been helpful writing songs with me at times in Seattle. If something significant didn't take off for me in regard to music, I would return to Seattle.

. . . .

I now focused my attention on the music producers: creative, sophisticated, nouveau riche. Jean Pierre, the "kingpin" producer, happened to own a successful locksmith business down the street from my hotel, right next door to the laundromat. I was baffled that a seemingly hip guy, who had mentioned more than once that he had recorded Marvin Gaye and Ray Charles, would have such a plebian business. Maybe he needed me to help him get famous again, and then he could help me.

Jean Pierre was seriously committed to his slender American girlfriend and their beloved German shepherd, Idris. Everyone smoked way too many Marlboros, except the dog, who only enjoyed the secondhand smoke. And when we couldn't think of anything to say, Jean Pierre would light up a cigarette that he had filled halfway with hashish, which he would share with anyone showing interest.

Jean Pierre and Leslie were an unlikely but well-matched couple. They lived in an enviable apartment at the top of Montmartre overlooking Paris. Their living room was circular with curved windows offering a panoramic view, complete with a high-powered telescope. I asked if they ever spied on their neighbors; they assured me they never did, although it would be very easy to do.

"Julie, you ask such funny questions," Jean Pierre quipped.

"When I ask funny questions, I get funny answers," I replied, hoping to stir up some humor.

I think that went over their heads, as they were somewhat conservative, but I wasn't sure due to all that hashish in the Marlboros.

I loved that it was so easy to have appreciative, cool, well-to-do friends. As we got to know each other better, they learned I was living in the modest Hôtel Caulaincourt and suggested I stay instead in a condo they had recently purchased as an investment. It was located down from the Sacré-Coeur on rue du Chevalier de la Barre.

The condo was unfurnished, so they provided me with the basics: a table and two chairs, a double mattress, bedding, dishes and pans, a corkscrew, and a couple of glasses. I was set. This sure beat the hotel— and it was located in the enchanting neighborhood of Montmartre! They graciously offered that I stay for a few months for free while I was working on the lyrics for their compositions. My friend Mia, who'd been attending the Sorbonne, was flabbergasted that I was able to find such an ideal place to live so soon. She called it "Julie's bachelorette pad." It was perfect for me, with shutters on all the windows that I opened wide every morning to let the exquisite Parisian sunlight pour in. At night, I would close them for total quiet and privacy. When new acquaintances came by, I would open the shutters and sing down to them: "I'd like to get to know you, yes I would . . . I'd like to get to know you if I could," as they gazed up at me laughing, "Julie, your life is a musical!" It was beginning to feel that way.

Rue du Chevalier de la Barre was a historic street, and cab drivers were impressed. They had no trouble bringing me home at night. During this heady point in Paris, I hardly gave a thought to my former life in Seattle. By this time I was hanging out in jazz clubs, singing sporadically, and making new, interesting friends and connections. I didn't imagine that the carefree, joyous life I was living would ever end. With the offer of staying in their condo, I let Tor know I would remain in Paris for a couple more months. Tor was thrilled for me and looking forward to visiting at Christmas.

How often does such a *coup de chance* (stroke of luck) happen in one's life at just the right moment?

I was on a roll, though a bit naive and floored about being in Paris. I was the perfect foil for people like these nouveau riche entrepreneurs.

They had plenty to offer me, especially an introduction to recording. Since all this was in exchange for my talent, which I wasn't yet positive I had, I felt I got the better end of the deal. And Jean Pierre and Leslie seemed to think that I was the goose that laid the golden egg; I didn't want to reveal to them that I might not be the next Madonna. I also imagined we would be forever friends.

Being abroad is a great opportunity to discover other ways to live. In Paris, I didn't have my controlling "familial support system" distracting me from my two objectives there: to cultivate a successful singing career and to learn French.

Now that I had my own apartment for a few months, two producers, and reliable friends, I had to produce some lyrics. The problem was how to begin to take my talent for humorous songwriting, which I'd done in the past, more seriously. My old songs had been crafted casually and mainly for quick laughs, not for public scrutiny. Now I needed a sharper edge for fashioning my complexities. I needed creative collaboration.

Jean Pierre had a state-of-the-art recording studio in his home where he said he had recorded albums with Ray Charles and Marvin Gaye. This was an alluring combination of fairy tale and a potential dream come true, and it worked for me within the vibrancy of Paris and my friendship with them. I didn't want to ask too many questions and appear apprehensive.

I was never quite sure if the stories people told me here were true, but in Paris magical things were often afoot. I chose to suspend my disbelief until I heard something different.

At the same time, I was cultivating my personal repertoire of interesting, retro jazz standards as I pondered where and how to find the audience for that genre of music. There were so many fantastic songs already written that I wanted to learn and sing.

I earnestly penned several avant-garde, angst-ridden lyrics to their convoluted disco compositions. The problem, I suspected, was that they were writing formulaic music that might become a "hit," so it lacked the essence of artistry I needed.

I entitled one song "Silent Whipping." The music had a consistent beat like the cracking of a whip. "Whip It" by Devo was constantly on the radio and at dance clubs. I denied that I might be unconsciously plagiarizing their song. I was trying to create edgy lyrics with hints of quirky sadomasochism. I was embarrassed to sing the lyrics in front of the producers, but they didn't care. They had the expensive recording equipment and an artsy American writing and singing the lyrics. Why shouldn't it be a hit? Apparently, they liked my unique contribution.

I felt comfortable with the producers but not excited about what I was singing. I would have liked it if a more down-to-earth person like Jordan was part of this scene; he was genuinely a writer, intelligent and articulate. These guys were impractical, with visions of easy mega success. I sensed they had unrealistic expectations of themselves, as well as me.

While I sang my lyrics in the recording booth, Jean Pierre directed me, raising his arms in the air, as if he were conducting a rock concert in a huge stadium. Sometimes his clenched fists were striking invisible targets around him while he yelled, "Give it your all, Julie! Go all the way, take it to another level!"

I wanted to ask, "What level do you mean?" If I could have delivered it, I would have. But I did not know how to do that on command and the music wasn't reaching me in a compelling way.

At that point in my career, I was not a singer-songwriter, but I wanted to be. It's natural to eventually write your own songs as a singer. I accepted any musical offers and used them as a form of rising to the occasion and growing as an artist. The producers were foreigners in my eyes, and seemed to have no idea how lame my lyrics actually were—or did they?

I have heard that anything worth doing is worth doing badly. How else are you going to get better? These lyrics were not good, but they had potential. The producers recorded all the songs I wrote lyrics for. One was about being a lady truck driver (I wrote it with Madonna in mind, as I knew she'd turn it into a hit); the most ludicrous song was about a fanatic young Englishwoman who was obsessed with Prince Philip of England. (I had Cyndi Lauper in mind for that one.)

The producers were desperate and determined to get a hit out of me, and I felt they would not release me until they had one. I wrote about my life experiences, but my lyrics didn't resonate with their music, and there was a lack of chemistry in our attempts at collaboration. I didn't feel comfortable saying anything. I was enjoying my bachelorette pad on Rue du Chevalier de la Barre. They were respectful and kind without demanding too much. They were as lost in this realm of songwriting "hits" as was I.

Not quite sure how to handle the situation, I sensed that a foreboding end to this dubious endeavor was looming in the near future, so I ended up saying goodbye to my adorable apartment in the hills of Montmartre when, out of the blue, another opportunity fell into my lap.

9. Gunila, Velkommen

My life is perfect, even when it's not.
— Ellen DeGeneres

As an American singer with uncertain potential, in Paris in the '80s, I realized that people who didn't know me had a "colorful" perception of me—even though so far only a few people in Paris had heard me sing. I was a mystery I believed they wanted to solve. For instance, I could be mistaken as a freewheeling foreign woman seeking romantic adventures. Or the inexplicable, odd visiting artist who might turn into the next famous singer on the charts, and they happened to know her! Or someone difficult to categorize, so they simply rolled their lips, making a sound like a quiet motorboat.

I interpreted their perception positively. As if I were a mind-boggling conglomeration of American pop culture they had yet to experience. I was whoever they thought I was. I enjoyed this porous, temporary role, depending on the situation. Life took place in real time on the streets of Paris. If they wanted fantasy, I was happy to let them believe the incredible.

For my first months in Paris, I occasionally found myself attending *vernissages* (art openings), displaying an artist's new works in a titillating milieu, including intoxicating beverages and snacks. These affairs brought out the beautiful, the rich, and anyone interested in viewing art and drinking for free.

In early December 1983, after a two-week singing gig aboard a cruise ship in the Canary Islands, I returned to Paris and found myself at one of these events. It was here that I became acquainted with a painter from the States, Daniel Cueva, a cross between Andy Warhol and Picasso. That particular evening, a crowd of Daniel's friends from England, Australia, and Paris were chatting. During my introduction to the gaggle surrounding him, between mouthfuls of wine and cheese, someone chimed, "You are American?" (We, as a nation, used to be much more attractive overseas than we are now.)

"Yes, and I sing jazz!" I exclaimed. I was proud of that, and it was the truest thing about me, as far as I was concerned.

"Fantastic, then you have got to meet Gunila [pronounced goo-NEE-la]—that is, if you don't *already* know the famously well-connected Swede! She loves expats and has great parties!"

He opened his little black book to read me her phone number, and I wrote the information on a scrap of paper and memorized it. (*Julie, don't lose that number.*) She sounded like the next person I needed to meet. I wanted to cultivate a cadre of happening, open-minded, multilingual personalities. And I thrived at parties.

I called her and she seemed happy to hear from me. She insisted she wanted to see me, so we arranged a rendezvous at her home. The '80s in Paris was a belle epoque when expats like Gunila were living there and openly welcomed foreigners into their lives, homes, and parties, which is exactly how life should be.

She lived near the Sacré-Coeur, on Rue Custine, at the top of a well-kept brick apartment building. She wasn't working that day, and I just happened to be extremely available. I timidly entered the tiny elevator, wondering what on earth I might be getting into this time.

Gunila opened the door wide with a gracious "Velkommen!" I was instantly seduced by the deeply eroded laugh lines encasing her translucent bluish eyes that complemented her radiant smile. She wore no makeup and had a mop of strawberry-blond hair. I saw a smart, grown-up hippie, an adult Pippi Longstocking—my kinda gal.

We sat down to delicious mugs of soothing valerian tea, used commonly for relaxation, along with a Swedish-style dessert plate of spicy gingersnaps. Smiling, she was eager to hear my story and to share some of hers. I embraced her hygge quality of Scandinavian hospitality, her ability to cultivate quaint aesthetics of warmth and hospitality to an art.

Gunila had a day job as an X-ray technician. In her free time, she also practiced Reiki. As I grew to trust her bohemian ways, we became friends.

She was a one-woman United Nations party. She loved to open her top-floor apartment with its partial view of the city to friends and acquaintances from all over the world. She was known for holding a memorable Christmas Eve celebration. If you were lucky enough, you'd be invited to it. The timing might be perfect if I ended up staying till then.

Gunila had a penchant for shadowy, mysterious African men and "married" several of them at different times. The ceremonies were held in her apartment, with incense and strange, soup-like concoctions bubbling on the stove. Being the ultimate libertine, laid-back Scandinavian, she was more than willing to live outside the box. She was like the older, wilder sister I thought I needed but never had.

She was successful at being a free spirit with strong boundaries and wasn't afraid to say what was on her mind. I liked it. I wasn't used to that. But with Gunila I knew where I stood, if nothing else.

As people arrived at her apartment she'd tell them, "This is a shoeless house, and if you don't like it, you don't come in." She had a row of eclectic slippers of every size and style outside her door as well as a long bench where people could sit to take their shoes off.

I was looking around for a new place to live in Paris, since my return from the cruise—sometimes staying in a hotel, and other times crashing with friends who had a couch to spare.

"If it will help out, why don't you stay here for one week and only one week?" Gunila offered. I thought that was generous, and since I was in a hotel that preferred guests be temporary, it was time to move on.

I took her up on her offer. She let me know that she expected me to look for work as a singer, and I mean *work hard* at it. She gave me names of a few clubs to check out, even though I had my own system of looking for gigs. I think she simply didn't want me hanging around her place every night. Finding a good gig was my reason for being in Paris.

I met her friends and went to jazz performances and galleries. She told everyone I was looking for a singing engagement. We talked about all kinds of things, including the adventure of being involved in music. I preferred the comfort of her home over a hotel. I even made efforts at finding gigs that my heart wasn't into. I admit I was a bit lax about looking for a new gig since I had been working on that cruise. I didn't want just any singing engagement. I wanted one where I fit in, people loved me, and it was happening. Was that too much to ask? I was at a turning point and considering returning to Seattle before too long. When it got down to it, in two and a half months in Paris I hadn't found a place where I really thought I could sing. It was easy to fall into the lifestyle of parties, art galleries, and dinners with new friends, but that frivolous life eventually lacked a certain substance. I wanted to sing in a club where I could be regularly seen and heard—a steady gig so I could start the ball rolling. Then I'd make even more interesting contacts and friends, I reminded myself. (*Attention, Julie: There are many fruitful rewards to working.*)

One miserable, rainy night, just a few days into my "visit" with Gunila, she kicked me out of her snug, comfortable apartment to go check out a brand-new club and restaurant that had advertised in the local paper they were looking for "acts." We'd both read about it, and I knew instinctively this would not be my kind of place. I resisted her suggestion.

"Gunila, I'm not sure that's the kind of venue where my 'act' would be appreciated."

"Julie," she replied, "how do you know if you don't try? You must go meet the people and find out. Maybe they can tell you about another club?"

I tried to explain to Gunila that I needed a jazz room where music was the focus and the surroundings were somewhat intimate—an established place known for having quality music. I felt like I was having a conversation with my grandmother from Norway. She didn't get it but was giving plenty of unasked-for advice and commands.

She wouldn't accept my not checking it out. She felt I was making excuses just because the weather was wretched. She questioned that maybe I felt "too good" to go check it out. She may have been right. But I sensed an underlying tension, signaling that Gunila meant business. It felt like "either go out and look for a gig or stay home and get a cold shoulder from the Swedish white witch!" I took the high road, wanting to keep my hostess happy.

Out into that cold, wet night I went—alone and scared. I caught the metro and within minutes I arrived on the Left Bank at Place Saint-Michel. It had stopped raining and the air felt fresh. It seemed implausible to just walk into a club alone like that and ask about a gig. But how do you explain to someone who isn't in show business that you have your own ideas about where you want to sing? I did not wish to alienate Gunila. At the moment, she was one of the best friends I had, even though bossy and someone who easily got on my nerves. She was probably kicking me out of the nest—I realized—so she could see one of her African "husbands" in private. I didn't blame her.

Reading the advertisement for this club again, as now I had it in my hand, I knew it wasn't the kind of venue that would go for my style: zany, sophisticated, subtle cabaret and jazz singer, loaded with innuendos. I was an entertainer who, while singing, would subtly include theatrics and act out songs. I wanted the audience to feel they were almost watching a movie.

Walking the lonely, wet streets of Place Saint-Michel, I approached the hollow, cavernous, bad idea of a hotspot I might want to be singing in. Since I'd made the effort, I went in. Every light was on, and not a soul was visible.

I sighted a woman sitting alone at a table for two. She was a little older than me. (Those were the days, when people were older than me!) She was attractive in that French, *tres soignée* (very neat) way, with her hair pulled back into a perfect chignon that she wore unselfconsciously. She had a wistful vibe and an open smile, so I asked her, *"Excusez moi, où sont les gens ce soir?"* (Where are the people?) in my broken French. She responded with *"Personne."* Which, confusingly, means "No one."

I explained that I was looking for the manager, and to justify why, I said, "I'm trying to find a singing engagement here!" (Was it just me, or did that sound pathetic? Why would anyone venture out on such a windy, wet night looking for a singing engagement? Was I doing this to keep peace with Gunila? Yes.)

This lovely Frenchwoman implied she didn't know where anyone was. Why should she? She was drinking a cup of tea and most likely waiting for a friend.

Surprisingly friendly, she invited me to sit down. I had nothing better to do, so I did.

We settled naturally into chatting. She was from the South of France, Aix-en-Provence, known for its lavender fields. She spoke an educated English with that alluring French accent. We told each other why we happened to be in Paris. It was comforting to meet someone like her on this unwelcoming night. Her story cautiously unfolded, of her being in love with a man, and something painful kept them apart: he was married and lived in another part of France with his wife, but they rendezvoused in Paris.

"He's married?" I asked incredulously.

I remember, as a younger woman, that seemed to be something I would never consider! What an ineffective way of finding love!

The woman engaged me with her kind curiosity and intelligent questions. I felt calm, being around her quiet energy. As we lost track of time conversing, the evening turned out to be a wonderful experience of revealing our souls to each other. She gave me her address and phone number in the South of France, and I held on to it for a long time, but I eventually lost track of her, partially because I couldn't decipher her handwriting. I don't even remember her name, but I do remember that she gave me the gift of kindness and transmitted a belief in me that, though understated, was complicit. (I may have forgotten the names of people I met, but I've never forgotten their generosity of spirit.)

Finally, a worried manager appeared. My friend explained to him in her exquisite French that I was an American jazz singer looking for a place to perform. I suddenly felt like I had an agent! Going out alone tonight felt like a great move! Gunila wasn't so wrong after all.

The manager explained that they were currently looking for a large, loud, rock-and-roll band. (*Why did I know that?*) I could certainly sing rock and roll, but that wasn't my thing.

My new friend and I continued talking, losing track of time. It seemed we were similar souls. She waited with me for a taxi and informed the driver exactly where I was staying. In the opposite direction, she walked toward the train station; it felt sad to say goodbye to my new friend. It was now after midnight.

When I returned to my current crash pad, Gunila was sleeping in the arms of her latest African husband on the living room floor in front of a smoldering fire. (Apparently, his African wife had given him the night off.) His arms were dark and sinewy in the warm light, and Gunila looked like a lifeless Cabbage Patch doll. Musk, incense, candles, and spicy orange fragrance lingered delicately in the air. She'd gone all out for her guy.

Every room was a sort of makeshift bedroom at Gunila's place. I crawled off to sleep in my comfy ordained guest room, happy that I'd ventured out on this inhospitable night. Because I persevered, I met another magical individual who fortified my momentum to remain on my path, and hopefully the right place would eventually reveal itself to me. I realized that what I wanted to find might not be easy, fast, or where I thought it might be. It might be a huge, astonishing surprise.

10. Paying My Dues in Polka-Dot Shoes

* * * * * * * * * * * * *

*The winds of God's grace are always blowing.
It is for us to raise the sails.*
— Ramakrishna

IT WAS IN SEATTLE THAT I FIRST DISCOVERED jam sessions, the most natural way to meet musicians, work on material, and make musical connections. These mysterious music laboratories were located in various dark tawdry bars and roadside cocktail lounges. Varied levels of musicianship were welcomed to play, from the apprehensive beginner to the potential virtuoso wanting to try new material. For musicians, they're valuable, a method of measuring one's progress and in developing stage presence.

So in Paris, that's exactly what I set out to do, and found them exotic and friendly. Musicians from all over the world converged in Paris, and if it was a lucky night, and they were free, it was possible to meet them. They talked about the music scene, where it's happening and where it isn't, what clubs are fun to play in and the ones to avoid. I availed myself of these conversations because I wanted to start warbling regularly, keeping up my singing chops, my chutzpah, and that elusive *je ne sais quoi* (which I seemed to have more than enough of).

Paris was a perfect place to reinvent myself. No one would be the wiser since no one knew me. I hardly knew myself. I realized it was my job to work on my personal "image and self-concept." The time had come for me to be responsible for all sorts of things about myself that I used to rely on others for. In my recent past I hadn't focused on "me" as a concept. In the beginning of my career I just put myself out there on various stages in a multitude of venues to see how my talent and presentation organically bubbled up, figuring that would tell me who I was. Now I wondered what would happen if I actually gave strategic thought to this process?

At low points, I wondered if I had enough of what it took to really go down this road. Was singing and entertaining a legitimate enough career for me to flourish in? Norman, my older brother, a classical pianist, had taken that more legitimate path, so I followed in kind. Only I was a fun-loving, humorous cabaret and jazz singer.

In the small town of Seattle in the '80s, there wasn't much cabaret culture, which is a collaborative, oftentimes humorous combination of theater and music in a restaurant/bar setting. I didn't realize it, but I was creating my own brand of cabaret in Seattle. Sporadic work in my hometown combined with a fair amount of recognition caused me to wonder if I was a square peg squeezing my sassy self into a round hole. I'd sing for a while, and then feel compelled to get a "real job" as a receptionist in an office, because gigs were so unpredictable. I'd try to juggle both, but after a late night singing, an early morning temp job was a recipe for disaster. But I did it anyway. I didn't realize it, but I needed an escape hatch from Seattle. And I thank Tor for seeing this in my future.

While I explored my singing career in Paris, Tor was making lots of money in some remote part of the Bering Sea fishing, as well as encouraging me to expand my singing engagements. There was nothing he wanted more than to eventually visit me in Paris and proudly watch his girl singing to the French in all her dazzling glory.

Those late nights I spent as a kid falling sleep to Frank Sinatra on the stereo paid off in Paris. I learned the standards and Great American Songbook through osmosis, and in Paris I translated and sang them in French. "What Is This Thing Called Love?" *(Qu'est-ce que c'est l'amour?)*

Because a talent to entertain came easily, I discounted its value. I didn't consider all the time and effort I took in putting myself together, hitting the streets in search of clubs, networking with strangers to build an audience, and sometimes auditioning. Then being told, "We're booked for the year"; it's easy to overlook the subconscious cost of rejection.

In Paris, I mailed off promotional materials, including publicity photos and my demo cassettes, to clubs and agencies. I wondered if they were ever received. And would people who received them know what to do with them if they were? Maybe the recipients didn't speak English? I didn't speak enough French to even negotiate a gig. I awaited a response, hoping someone who spoke some English might call with an enticing offer. I told myself this was all part and parcel of the rituals one performs for the muse, and the learning curve in the music business while in Paris.

I kept telling myself, *I have to work harder*. I was constantly learning new songs, branching out linguistically through memorizing French lyrics and choosing challenging material, like Jacques Brel's "Ne Me Quitte Pas" and Edith Piaf's "Milord." I found a mentor—a kindly, intellectual saxophonist and teacher, Jacques, who often played at the jams. We'd spend hours working on translations for jazz standards, and he'd help me with the pronunciation and meaning. Jacques occasionally sketched out musical charts so I could grow my repertoire with tunes like "Peel Me a Grape" and "I'm Hip." Night and day, my radar was up for music clubs and new songs. That became my ritual in Paris.

I was always searching for the perfect song, hoping my rendition would be the one to turn the tide, to catch the ear of an influential person who happened to be in the audience or to open my promo package. Someone could decide they wanted me to be in their show. Pursuing my career felt like a sort of gambling addiction. Memorizing lyrics was a high priority for me, so that I could internalize the song completely. I wrote the lyrics on the palm of my hand or on index cards and carried them in my pockets, and whenever I had to take the metro or wait for anything, I'd take them out and study. I felt like a human jukebox. If I were getting paid the big bucks, I could rationalize the time and discipline it took to memorize a song. But I loved the songs I memorized, and now I'd have them forever.

Did I really want this? Apparently so, as I rarely questioned it. At times, becoming frustrated with lack of work, I threatened (myself) to quit the music biz. But I thought, *And do what?* There was nothing else I wanted more than to perform, and if I got a chance, I was good at it. That's where I felt the most alive and in touch with my essence. There was a lot to learn about the business side, but I definitely had a penchant for music and song. If I became successful—not necessarily famous, just highly requested—it would be worth it.

As best I could, I turned every one of my living situations into my music studio/office where I'd practice with my tape deck, organize sets of songs that created a certain dynamic, and make cold calls from a list of clubs and managers I'd heard of. I kept doing this, although it felt pointless and like rejection. I thought, *Perhaps I'm too glamorous for the venue,* or *My style isn't to their taste* (even though I was more than ready to morph into anything they wanted me to be, if they asked). I was getting used to a fair amount of refusal—even expecting it. The music business is filled with assorted rejections and then, when you least expect it, there's that one yes!

The sudden reopening of a recently closed club provided a surprising opportunity. I had an appointment at two o'clock that afternoon with Benoit the manager, who was head over heels excited to hire an American jazz singer. He introduced me to the bleary-eyed house pianist, Richard. Disheveled and rummy, he looked like it was too early in the day for him to be anywhere. He accepted an espresso with several lumps of sugar from the manager and assured me he could read jazz charts.

"But can you play the blues in B-flat?" I asked, as he lit up his second cigarette before putting out the first.

"I've been playing zee blues all my life," he mumbled.

I handed him a few standards I thought he'd feel familiar with. The following Saturday night would be my first paid gig in Paris, from 9 to 11p.m. I had two days to prepare. It wasn't an established club or the kind of place I envisioned singing in Paris. It looked more like an American-style basement rec room, located in the Bastille. The upright piano had seen better days. The bar was L-shaped with three stools and plentiful bottles of spirits. The main room was cluttered with a smattering of old cabaret tables and chairs and several colossal pillars blocking the view for the attendees who happened to get a table near one.

I was excited but also thought to myself, *Gee, it was oddly easy to get this gig.*

I decided to make the night memorable and wear my beaded blue dress by Seattle designer Malorie Nelson. I had the wacky idea to wear a contrasting red leather "biker" jacket that Tor had given me as a going-away present. It wasn't quite the right ensemble, but I went with it, as I wanted to show Paris some of Seattle's treasures.

At show time, there was a smattering of patrons in the room. I opened with an upbeat version of Judy Garland's "Almost Like Being in Love," recalling, at one time, how I believed this song set the bar for all love songs to come. I was addicted to love songs.

As the pianist stumbled throughout the tune (I noticed the second page had fallen on the floor), I tried to pick it up but the beaded number would not allow it. To boost my confidence I closed my eyes and thought about my polka-dot shoes. Opening my eyes, I observed, *Gee, there's a couple at a table, smiling. I wonder if they're laughing at the absurdity that there's a singer dressed in a designer gown, and a biker jacket and polka-dot shoes, singing her heart out to a nearly nonexistent audience. Oh, well, I'm getting paid,* I hoped. The pianist was missing notes and a few teeth that I thought were supposed to be there. Considering it was our first night and he'd probably never played that song before, I cut him a lot of slack.

I began to sashay my hips, hoping to distract and amuse the audience. I felt exposed. The room was bright—for some reason no one had dimmed the house lights for ambiance on this legendary evening in Paris! A bar is supposed to create a mood, so listeners can fall into a trance, believe in love again, forget their sorrows, and become happy. At least while the singer entertains them with "Fly Me to the Moon."

A few more patrons sauntered in and glanced my way as if wondering what I was doing there. They sat down to talk to each other and barely listened to me. I didn't blame them; in such a place, I probably wouldn't listen to me either. One man at the bar was actually sleeping, with his head cradled in his arms. He'd been there earlier but fell asleep when I started singing. Was I that boring?

There are plenty of singing engagements that are painfully unforgettable, but this was my beginning in Paris—shouldn't it have been more spectacular? I guess I had to jump into the pool at the shallow end. One has to start somewhere in a new town. Benoit stood in the back of the club, smiling and toasting me with his drink. At least he liked me.

Finding a consistent gig at a great club I could call home was my dream. I felt it would lead to the confidence I needed to transform myself into a hyper-glamorous singer in long white gloves and designer gowns. I'd be entertaining full houses of enthusiastic revelers from all over the world several nights a week. Everybody from everywhere would come to Paris to fall in love with me! A heady nightly project! Yes, that was my vision. Unfortunately, this club was in need of more attention than I was capable of giving.

While I was singing, the idea crept up: *Have I undersold my talent?* I gave that audience what they could handle. Singing is a learning experience. On this particular night, anything extra would have gone unappreciated. Much to Benoit's chagrin, I did not return. There had to be something better.

11. American Church in Paris

You meet your destiny on the road you take to avoid it.
— Jean de la Fontaine

THE AMERICAN CHURCH WAS IN A PRIME LOCATION near the Eiffel Tower and the Seine. The church's main attraction was its helpful bulletin board, where you found *les petites annonces* (want ads). This bulletin board was famous in the expat community as an effective place to find short-term rentals and sublets, employment, and various items for sale or donation. I was looking for a part-time job teaching English or a cat-sitting gig in exchange for free rent. The songwriting position had run its course.

That particular early winter's day, I noticed the pleasant feeling of increasing comfort and familiarity in Paris—kind of like, *This could get to be my turf.*

As I perused the message board, an unanticipated gift appeared on the steps in the foyer of the church.

Sitting quietly, watching people come and go, was a strange little man with a twinkle in his eyes. He was dressed like a genie, having recently been traveling through Yemen, and was now in Paris, the bearer of good tidings. The only thing missing was a Persian carpet and magic lamp. He was a traveler like myself, only he wore comfortable, shapeless clothing and I was doing my best to feel stylish and not embarrassed in my too-tight blue jeans.

A generous vagabond happy to help a less experienced traveler, he told me his name was Joel and asked the usual questions about why I was in Paris and what was I looking for. Once you've been generously helped, then you freely offer the same to others. It's the "code" and way of the wanderers, like angels of providence. And I loved that generous way of being with others.

He knew more about Paris than I and willingly answered all my questions—like where I might find a quick bite to eat in this neighborhood. I was getting hungry and it was definitely a high-end district with the Eiffel Tower in plain view. Once out of the metro, I had noticed every bistro window I looked in had white tablecloths and signs saying Reservation Nécessaire. He directed me to a crêperie, which I planned to check out after the *petites annonces*.

When I disclosed the charmed phrase "I'm a jazz singer and looking for places to do my thing," he lit up. Then he said something that struck me to the core. A *coup de chance* (a cup of good luck)!

"If you're a singer, you've got to meet a guy named Stacy Macadams. He is the musical director for an American-styled club, which is unusual for Paris and very popular. He plays piano for all the singers and singing waiters. There's a jazz group with a singer. It is really wild and called the Hollywood Savoy."

As I listened, I just kept nodding and saying inside, *Yes, go on, go on—I'm really liking this conversation, except the part about singing waiters!*

"Take the metro to the Bourse," he told me as he munched an apple he had taken out of his patchwork cloth sack. "It stops in front of the Bourse—the French stock exchange. The restaurant is across the street. You can't miss it."

Now, that was a mouthful of valuable information for a first conversation! I practically inhaled it, writing the name and address in my little red address book.

"Merci beaucoup!" I was grateful and wanted to give him one of the friendly, polite kisses that seemed to be au courant in Paris, but since neither of us were French, I opted out. "I'll tell Stacy you sent me."

I hoped this wouldn't be another wild goose chase—something musicians and performers are used to.

"It'll be great when you meet him!" His eyes glowed.

I thought, *Finally a real possibility! A cool club to check out.* The Hollywood Savoy had a groovy-sounding name. I passed up the crêpe stand heading for the metro, definitely on a mission. As long as there was daylight, I wanted to follow up on the lead. There was nothing more important I had to do than get a fantastic gig.

I was grateful that Le Bourse was indeed the name of the metro stop, and that the Hollywood Savoy was located in all its splendor across the street from it. His directions were good, and I had paid close attention this time. There it was, a high-end-looking club/restaurant that would have fit perfectly in New York or Los Angeles. The classic awnings surrounded full windows that you couldn't really see into because of the glare of the afternoon sun. The gold calligraphy on the window of the place told me I was entering an established venue filled with endless possibility.

I stepped into the club not knowing what might happen but wondering if my career might suddenly take on a shiny new veneer.

I was a little apprehensive about singing waiters, a concept that was passé in Seattle—but apparently it wasn't in Paris. At one time, I had tried my hand at this abysmal trend when I graduated from college. I was a lousy waitress, and then I'd try to make it up to the distraught diners with a winning song and a strong, beautiful voice.

The Great American Food & Beverage Company was one of Seattle's most successful restaurants. Since I had to accompany myself on the guitar, one of my simple hits was "Help Me Make It through the Night" (a subconscious cry for help with my career?). During an overwhelming Mother's Day brunch, I alone served a family of eight everything except what they specifically asked for: pancakes, omelets, gigantic cinnamon rolls, and lasagna. Then, as the ultimate climax for this dissatisfied family affair, I began singing, "Take the ribbon from my hair, shake it loose and let it fall…." The mother gasped, as if hearing such a song was the last straw!

I felt painfully inappropriate, in my revealing, bust-enhancing company shirt, while my heart was beating faster than was good for me. Was I a flop? Being both a server and an entertainer at the same time was too much for me. I couldn't wait for my shift to be over.

Still feeling that dread of returning to a job I was not cut out for, I dutifully showed up the next day and got the news only by seeing my name removed from the schedule. Singers were standing in line to work there. I promised myself I would *never do that again*.

Singing waiters could be unique and trendy for Paris, but it was definitely not my style. I was onto something much bigger in Paris. Magic was afoot!

12. Discovering the Hollywood Savoy

. . . .

Something in me knows where I'm going.
— Jackson Pollock

AFTER THE FORTUITOUS MEETING with the helpful world traveler at the American Church, I was eager to pick up on his hot tip. I had been in Paris for two months, and I had recently changed my round-trip ticket to make the return date open-ended; things were percolating with the recording and songwriting. Although that hadn't really gone anywhere, it gave me a stable place to live for two months and added to my experience with professional tapes of my original recordings. Paris was creatively welcoming on different levels: I was discovering more opportunities to sing jazz and accepting the gentility of the French, plus I felt happy, as if I were living in a surreal, magical village designed for artistic dreamers.

Now on an undertaking to meet the music director, Stacy Macadams, at the Hollywood Savoy, I hustled my bustle to sniff out this prospect. I had to see what this American-styled floor show in Les Halles was all about. I recalled that's exactly how I'd described myself on my handmade publicity announcements in Seattle: "Julie Cascioppo—she's an act, she's a floor show, a one-woman wonder you can wonder about."

It was about five o'clock when I stepped tentatively into the Hollywood Savoy. A faint aroma of cigar smoke, a provocative perfume, and something mouthwatering wafting from the kitchen permeated the atmosphere, reminding me I hadn't had a healthy meal in a while. I was curious to discover who this Stacy *was*. It was a first, to actually meet the "music director" of a club. I wasn't in Seattle anymore.

I quickly spotted a handsome man, with an almost pretty face and a full head of silky brown curls, gingerly tossing them out of his eyes while rehearsing with an up-and-coming opera singer performing the theme song from the film Diva, a current smash hit. Her voice was notable, and I hoped I wasn't too far out of my league. The singing waiters were reviewing their music while simultaneously folding white cloth napkins and setting the tables for the dinner service. Though the club wasn't open for dinner yet, the work atmosphere was convivial. The variety of staff spoke a combination English and French. I sat at the bar, sitting up straighter than usual, hoping to grab someone's attention. Smiling as he walked toward me, Stacy welcomed me with a combination of Southern comfort and New York savoir faire.

"Good evening, I'm Stacy Macadams. And who might you be?" he asked, probably assuming I could be a homesick tourist looking for company or a singer in search of a gig.

"I'm Julie, a singer from Seattle. I met a fellow, Joel, at the American Church today and he said you might be interested in me. He says hello, by the way."

"I'm not sure I know Joel, but if he says he knows me, I must because I know all the characters in Paris."

Suave, sassy, and with a talent to amuse, Stacy was an elegant man. He sported a navy-blue double-breasted jacket and an ascot, his manner nonchalant as if showing me around his yacht. I couldn't imagine he really knew Joel, but apparently Joel knew him.

Being relentless, tenacious, and determined to find my place in this City of Light, I joyfully followed this lead to wherever it might take me.

"Julie, why don't you come back later, after nine when the place starts hopping? Bring your music, and I'll invite you up to sing." That was all I needed to hear. I had a number of songs I'd been working on. This could be the start of something big! On my way back to my hotel, I stopped off at my favorite falafel stand, savoring the scrumptious combination of flavors that became a satisfying meal for me.

Back at my hotel, I took a hot, relaxing bath in the petite bathtub. I was excited to get ready for the evening. Discreetly applying dark eyeliner, mascara, and a sizzling red lipstick, I was ready for anything. I dressed casual: black shiny slacks and a red lace camisole underneath my red-leather biker jacket. I hoped it was obvious I was looking for a gig, and had a feeling this venue could be a perfect fit. I wanted it to work out. *Hollywood Savoy, here I come.*

I told myself I could do anything, and on top of that, I'd been there once today. Now I was returning with music in my satchel and sparks of hope in my heart. Striding through the club's maroon-and-gold gilded doors, I hid the discomfort of being alone by chiding myself, *Get used to it for now, you just haven't found your entourage yet.*

I was bravely trying to enrich my life and have it make sense in one of the world's most vibrant cities—and it was only Tuesday night.

At 9:00 p.m. Stacy was settled at the piano while I sat at the bar observing and listening as he set the mood, playing a Rachmaninoff tour de force I hadn't heard since I was a child. When he finished the elaborate arrangement with a climactic glissando he greeted the audience, with a smarmy Liberace smile, "*Belle soirée mesdames et messieurs,*" commanding the audience's attention and hitting several octaves as he played glissandos up and down the grand piano, leaning into a stride, like the world-class impressario he was. "I am Stacy Macadams from Memphis, Tennessee, and . . . you are not." Again, he delivered his Liberace smile, then broke into a vigorous version of Gershwin's "Swanee" and "You Made Me Love You."

How utterly novel, I thought to myself. If it was good enough for Judy Garland, live at Carnegie Hall, it was good enough for Stacy. It seemed odd to hear a folksy song of the old South in Paris, but Stacy made it palatable with his humor and great big genuine smile.

I admired his jovial showmanship and uncanny ability to "work the crowd" as if he knew them personally. (Ah, the enthralling techniques I was absorbing through paying attention to him.)

Stacy laughed at his own jokes and everyone else's, which was part of his charm. He might as well have been saying, "Laugh, come on—I'm doing it!" He was tickled to by his own bon mots and equally appreciated the cleverness of others.

Stacy spoke with a Southern drawl and a New York edge, then sang tenor as if in a barbershop quartet. He didn't take anything too seriously, except the music and that the singers be in their "key light" (the spotlight at just the right angle that brings out the best in you). Whenever he took a brief break, he feverishly gulped a tall glass of water (Or was that vodka? One never knew). He'd be joking and on the verge of laughter and then abruptly begin to sing a heartbreaking interpretation of "Green, Green Grass of Home." When not at the piano he welcomed patrons entering the club as if it were his living room. He knew everyone's name, including those of the current American ambassador, Evan Galbraith, and his wife, Bootsie.

He reminded me of a honey-voiced crooner you'd discover at Café Carlyle on a night out in New York, playing piano and singing glib love songs to an indulgent, adoring crowd.

On this, my first evening, guests began arriving at this trendy hot spot, a "must" destination on any evening in Paris. Stacy walked off the stage to say hello and then to me he said, "Once the show begins, I'll find a perfect time to introduce you and bring you up to sing."

I gave him the music to "Embraceable You" in the key of E-flat. "I don't need that. It's one of my absolute favorite songs," he gushed. He knew the song well, and was known to sing it on occasion, but he hadn't heard the French version yet!

"I'll sing it in French," I chimed in.

Besides accompanying and mentoring the young, zealous waitstaff with a tinge of vaudeville-styled showmanship, he was a dynamic host for each eclectic evening of whimsical, unpredictable cabaret and some improvisation, all done with the finessing touch of a good musical director.

After performing his grand number by Irving Berlin, "I Love a Piano," Stacy wrangled the attractive mixed bag of singing waitstaff, each performing one song that reflected their personality—from Bessie Smith's "Kitchen Man" to Marlene Dietrich's "The Boys in the Back Room." Stacy staged his singers on various perches and pedestals: sitting on the bar, or sitting on a surprised customer's lap, or some other amusing position, including next to Stacy at the piano bench—always with a dramatic spotlight positioned artfully on each singer as they had a moment in their "key light." In between numbers, the waiters served cherries flambé—or everyone's birthday favorite, flaming Baked Alaska. Lots of things were flaming at the Hollywood Savoy! A waiter laughingly shared that one night, not long ago, a woman's hair caught on fire through ignoring the birthday candles as Stacy played and sang "Happy Birthday" like a trooper, never missing a beat. A quick-thinking waiter came to the rescue with a picher of water.

The singing waitresses came from all corners of the Western world, including Australia, with various heights and depths of talent. Stacy commandeered the singing abilities of both the staff and audience. Even customers had unrealized talent that hadn't been discovered till Stacy got them on stage singing.

Taking this in, I felt my heart expanding. This was an implausible, phantasmagorical festival of the absurd, almost laughable, yet the players were as committed as any performer on Broadway! I related to the freedom and spontaneity of letting a night take on its own life, with someone like Stacy as the ringleader. This was the kind of place I was looking for. It wasn't overly controlled like some shows in Paris.

I wasn't exactly sure where I might fit in, so far. But I knew there would be no turning back if I could just slip my stiletto in the door.

Suddenly, I heard Stacy's commanding announcement on the microphone: *"Attention, mesdames et messieurs,* ladies and gentlemen! A special guest, just arrived from Seattle, Washington!"

Could there be someone else besides me coming from Seattle? I wondered.

"Please give a chaleureux (warm) welcome to Miss Julie Cascioppo from Seattle, WashingTON."

Oh my God! He pronounced my name correctly! I'd become engrossed in the show and was secretly hoping he had forgotten about me. I had joined a group of revelers at a nearby table, instigated by the Buddha-like Moroccan Claude Senouf. My tablemates had no idea I was one of the "spontaneous acts" Stacy had prearranged. Through the galvanizing applause I found my way to the stage and entered the "performance zone," where I would transform into a woman in love, singing as if I had deeply felt such emotions at one time in my life. Suddenly, I would no longer be the insecure foreigner hanging out in dark clubs alone. I felt sanctioned to release the emotion of the song. I was about to become a worldly woman, savvy, sultry, and maybe even a little dangerous.

Stacy played a discreet introduction to the song, and I began, enunciating each word in French as if it were a kiss: *"Un baiser . . ."* I was excited to show off the sentiment of this song and that I could sing it in French.

I wondered why the audience was chuckling every time I sang *"un baiser."* In general I never minded hearing laughter—it was a familiar experience with my audiences in the States as I was known for my cabaret humor and satirical renditions of certain well-known songs. But I was a little taken aback, since this wasn't a particularly funny song, or was it? I continued, remembering that no one had laughed when I sang it back home.

Stacy accompanied me well. I felt like, *Wow, that was good to get through and make a connection with the audience.* I was flushed with excitement.

Exiting the stage, I blew a shy, showbiz kiss to the table I'd been sitting at.

As I stepped down, Stacy grabbed his microphone and came to center stage with: "Julie—from Seattle, Washington!" He revived the audience with his "Give it up for the singer one more time!" Their affable applause felt like an extra helping of appreciation. I was touched.

During intermission, I visited *la toilette,* where my soon-to-be new friend, Susie Robinson, a cheeky English singing waitress, explained to me that the word *baiser* means "to kiss," and when used as a verb *baiser* also means to literally participate in sexual intercourse. As I was touching up my lipstick, my mouth dropped, and Susie laughed exuberantly, leaving me alone to contemplate my faux pas. I had a feeling French was going to be a challenging but humorous language for me to perform with.

I was mortified! And now I understood why singers didn't readily sing the French translation. As I continued studying French, a Romance language, I noticed there were many innuendos with sexual connotations, hardly noticeable but inferred throughout the language. *(This could become my shtick in Paris!)*

When I returned to the table, Claude Senouf, with a huge smile, gestured to me that he was *proud* of me. He offered another *coupe de champagne*. His entourage members were complimentary and tipsy. Relieved that my unspoken "audition" was over, I basked in the glow of accomplishment. I hadn't expected so much ribald attention. Sometimes it's overwhelming to be adored.

Next, Stacy announced the Hollywood Savoy Sleazettes, a lively trio that at this time consisted of the singing waitress Susie Robinson, from London; Claudia Phillips, from Los Angeles; and Nancy Cotton, from Boston. They performed a version of "Leader of the Pack" with great backup harmonies, stylish outfits, and choreography. They followed that with "Girls Just Want to Have Fun," a current hit all over the world. I could see the joy in that kind of music. In fact, I silently wished I was singing pop hits. But I had chosen jazz—or had jazz chosen me? I loved that this club had a musical feeling of "anything goes." All sorts of buttons were pushed and genres were sung. I liked this place and thought it might just like me.

After a crazy houseful of applause, a sort of changing of the guard took place: the rock-and-roll group disappeared and three jazz musicians slithered up to the bandstand, finding their positions and arranging their music, with pianist Eddy Goldstein from New York, Gus Nemeth on bass, and Vic Pitts on drums. All three had landed in Paris from the States at different times for different reasons, and all stayed.

Then came the main event, starring the dazzling Rochelle Robertson of Los Angeles and her trio. Stacy set them up with over-the-top accolades as an introduction. The audience sat up and tuned in to listen to jazz.

Rochelle was collected and cool, naturally beautiful yet rustic and capable. She carried herself like a woman who knew how to move in any environment. Before Hollywood, she had grown up on a ranch in Oklahoma riding horses. The room took on a new vibe as the band began to swing to a Duke Ellington song, and Stacy disappeared, taking a well-deserved break. Rochelle wore an impressive backless dress from the '40s, and the drama unfolded. She sang with a laid-back, dark, husky tone, and a "devil may care" style, completely self-possessed. She was almost *talking* the song. The jazz trio accompanied her with a relaxed savoir faire. "It don't mean a thing if it ain't got that swing! Doo ah, doo ah, doo ah, doo ah!"

I chuckled to myself because, once the band started to solo, I thought, *Could someone please just hand her a nail file so she won't look quite so bored?* She snapped her fingers on beats 2 and 4 while leaning on the piano, staring at the pianist. She appeared to be dreaming. I wondered where her thoughts were taking her. Nothing seemed to penetrate her concentration, yet she wasn't trying to entertain. She did nothing other than embody the song and be the epitome of who she was, and people lapped it up.

Whatever it was she was doing, it worked. She radiated understated pizzazz and Hollywood class. I decided to stick around; this kind of show captivated me deeply. I studied her every move. I found her noncommittal style actually made her oddly compelling. Very *Hollywood*! Very not a drag queen (where I had learned my tricks of the trade). She evoked a mysterious spell.

I would be so the opposite if it were my gig, I fantasized. I would be ostentatious with heels, cleavage, body-conscious clothing, lots of bling and high-definition makeup. I'd be fueled on adrenaline and unpredictable humor and wisecracks. I would do everything I could to capture attention and entertain. One of my showbiz tricks that I used on people I knew had been to call out a particular man's name, accuse him of being my ex-husband, and asking if he was "trying to get back together again or what?" With microphone in hand, I had the power. Wandering off the stage, I might nonchalantly ask someone if they spoke French. If they replied *"Oui,"* I might respond, *"Oh la la! Tant pis"* (too bad) and then scurry off.

I found every audience interesting and thrived on riling them up and blowing their minds, by not being what they were used to, and I could hardly wait to do that in Paris. But I'd wait till I had my own "room." I wouldn't turn on the audacity right away. I would develop familiarity and rapport with the vibe of the audience. I intuitively knew the parameters and didn't divulge my mischief right away.

Rochelle didn't try to be anything; she just was. She ended as casually as she began. No big whoop. I was riveted by her subtle style. After her set, Stacy resurfaced and got the audience to give it up for Rochelle and the boys in the band. She disappeared and I made a note to become a friend of hers.

Stacy maintained the momentum by taking over at the piano, making good-natured fun of the audience. He'd point out the nouveau riche living in a suburb outside Paris. (They loved being recognized, not quite realizing they were being made fun of.) His comedic banter in a mixture of French and English was a cue to the waitstaff that the grand finale of the evening's entertainment was in sight. He began a rousing rendition of the "Battle Hymn of the Republic" and everybody was required to sing. I went with the flow while hoping I'd never be asked to do that again. For some unknown reason, it felt uncomfortable for me to sing with a group.

I knew I would continue to spend time there regardless of whether I got a gig or not. This was my kind of club.

13. Claude the Moroccan

Be bold, be bold, and everywhere be bold.
— Herbert Spencer

CLAUDE SENOUF—OR CLAUDE THE MOROCCAN, as I thought of him—was one of the captivating characters I met the first night I sang a song at the Hollywood Savoy. I noticed that, most random times I dropped by the Savoy, he was there as well. I never quite knew what made him so enamored with the place. I also wondered how wealthy he was. He seemed to have money to burn, was somewhat reliable, had a lot of time on his hands, and wanted to befriend me.

It was early December, less than two months into my Paris adventure, and Rochelle was taking more nights off than usual. Stacy asked me if I'd like to sporadically fill in for her when she was unavailable. I jumped at the chance. She had a swinging trio, and they were all American. They knew what I knew: jazz.

Claude loved jazz, and I enjoyed having a friend like him in the audience. He had a warm smile and loved to have a good time, often bringing an eclectic entourage.

He was a chubby cherublike man with a generous heart. He hinted at being a rich man's son. The night we met, he was sitting at the *"grande table de bonne chance"* (large table of good luck), up front and facing the stage.

Claude was a favored guest at any venue, a true hedonist with a pocketbook ready to spend. On that first night, he had invited me to join his table and offered me champagne, which was a rarity in the States but de rigueur in Paris. It might have been a ploy to inspire the singer to loosen up, possibly to be more entertaining, and to help her forget why she left America.

He resembled a character out of a Fellini film, spinning fantastic future scenarios of me singing at his favorite classic hotel, the Mamounia Hotel in Marrakech—my kind of fantasy. There were no romantic expectations from him and plenty of dreamy notions and creative plans. He implied he had some background in painting and later as a gallery owner—and now he was the proprietor of his own radio station! A Renaissance man.

After a few business dinner dates at famous restaurants on the Rue de Rivoli he offered me a paid position of on-air host of the late-night show on his "private radio station," K-LOV. I was interested in anything that could augment my career and keep me in the music game. Besides, I could use the cash. As long as I was trying out this new way of life, without Tor, I wanted to become self-sufficient, something I had uncertainties about attaining. My bank account was beginning to noticeably dwindle.

"*Une belle femme n'a jamais assez d'argent*" (A beautiful woman never has enough money), a stranger nonchalantly quipped as I collected francs from a cash machine on the street one night. *Touché,* I thought.

In college I'd had some experience at the radio station in Bellingham, where I actually interviewed Count Basie in the men's locker room after his concert. I shyly told him I was a singer, hoping to develop my career. He told me if I ever got to New York to give him a call. At that time in my professional development, I was insecure about calling myself a real singer. A few years after I graduated from college, I went to New York, clutching the crinkled, worn paper he'd written his phone number on. I called him, and I was so nervous on every level I talked myself out of meeting up with him. I couldn't even tell if he remembered me; I told myself he was out of my league. I've always wondered what might have taken place between us had I been bolder. (How often does Count Basie give someone his phone number?)

While in college, I used my radio press pass to connect with jazz pianist Chick Corea as well. After his concert, I went up on the stage as if I belonged there, to gush about how much I loved his music. Unable to hide the college-girl crush I had on him, I asked if I could give him a kiss. He was agreeable, but that was the last time I asked a man if I could kiss him. (Since then I realized if you have to ask, maybe you shouldn't.) I kissed his cheek, which was bold for this small-town Seattle girl.

In Paris, being a disc jockey sounded like something I'd take to naturally, since I'd been successful at it in college. Claude said all I'd have to do is play records and converse about music, which I thought I knew all about. He assured me there was nothing to it. It wouldn't matter what I said, French people would simply love my voice and love hearing me speak English as they drifted off to sleep. I was skeptical and thought that sounded a bit "smarmy" for a professional radio station. But figured I would decide on how to present myself once I understood what I was doing logistically within the sound booth.

The station was located in a run-down house in the sleazy, nightlife-drenched 9th arrondissement, in Pigalle. The way he'd described it, I thought there would be a staff or at least an engineer, but it was just me. Claude showed me the ropes, as if I'd just received a Suzy Homemaker oven and was about to add water to a cake mix, plug in the oven, and bake it. The reality was I wasn't sure what to do if anything went wrong while working an undesirable late-night shift, 11:00 p.m. to 2:00 a.m. I understood the turntable and how to play the selections he had made available. If I wanted to, he told me, I could select my personal favorites. That sounded easy. He added that I could say groovy things between the songs.

I tried my best. But I was out of my comfort zone and felt nervous to be alone there after Claude left. The dimly lit neighborhood was eerie and quiet in the late hour. Honestly, I was spooked. *Why had I agreed to do this?* (Risking my life for my career again, I reassured myself.)

"If you're nervous, my dear, just lock yourself inside and call me if anything comes up." He sounded like Leonard Cohen in his later years. I said, "Ah . . . thanks a lot, Claude."

He demonstrated how I could use my "sultry voice," imitating me: "Time for 'Round Midnight,' 'cause, it is . . . 'round midnight!" Now, how do you not find that appealing? I must have captured his imagination.

Luckily for me, it was only one night a week. And by the following week, I had enticed a friendly escort from my French class, my friend Joe, from Barbados, a future dress designer. He offered to help me out as a sort of bodyguard, and I was glad to have his company.

Claude was oblivious to the fact that, as a foreign woman alone, I was compromising my safety. Why was I so easily beguiled by magical thinking? Was it part of being an artist, to try things that logical people would never do? Was I so enmeshed in my fairy tale of improbable strategies that I could not seem to find what I really wanted to manifest?

14. Lavelle

. . . .

Never step on a diva's toes.
— Lavelle

AFTER SEVERAL WEEKS IN PARIS, I had an aha moment when I discovered *Pariscope*, the weekly "cultural bible" of the city, which was available at any kiosk where they sold daily newspapers and magazines. It became an invaluable guide to Paris nightlife. Also, musicians I met at the various clubs as well as Stacy Macadams encouraged me to go see Lavelle, a Black vocalist from Los Angeles whom Parisians thought was equal to Aretha.

She was the queen of jazz and rhythm and blues in the Paris club scene. If she invited you into her fold, you acquired a certain *je ne sais quoi* (I don't know what). With her recommendation of you, you got the gig at clubs where she was known and highly regarded.

She was in demand because she could do it all.

I first saw her at the famous jazz joint Aux Trois Mailletz. In 1983 it was slowly making a resurgence, having been hot in the 1950s but then fading to obscurity.

Now under new ownership, it was cultivating a casual but happening atmosphere and becoming known by singers as a place where they could hang out, sit in, or get a gig.

Located in Saint-Michel, on Rue Galande, an ancient, meandering cobblestone alley, riddled with historical nuance, it was an iconic jazz club referred to as a *"cave."*

At that time, Nina Simone occasionally performed at the same venue. Her second home was a hotel in the Latin Quarter.

To enter, one had to walk down a steep set of narrow stairs into a musty, difficult-to-breathe-in, humid, sweaty, cigarette-laden atmosphere, brimming with anticipation of discovering a musical spark. I could feel that nervous tension of revelers high on boozy cocktails thrilled to be out at night, thrown into the unknown, in a strange, otherworldly, time-warped cabaret from the '50s—like a scene from the American film *Funny Face* with Audrey Hepburn and Fred Astaire.

I watched Lavelle, spellbound. She was accomplished and polished. She nailed the technique of "belting" in musical parlance, a technique that some singers seem to be blessed with more than others. And she accompanied herself seamlessly on piano.

Due to their cachet and historical relationship with Paris, Black singers were often the preferred performers in clubs. I struggled with the question *Why do I even bother to sing in Paris, when they have Lavelle?* But, I slowly came to realize, I have other qualities.

Lavelle took a break and I decided to make my move sooner rather than later. I introduced myself (that took guts) and told her I loved her show, because I did. She was impressive. She had the audience in the palm of her hand, like I would want to if I had a gig in Paris. I mentioned I was new in town and that Stacy Macadams from the Hollywood Savoy had recommended I check her out. I let that sink in, adding that I was from Seattle. (She was duly unimpressed with my city, as was most anyone.)

I delicately launched into the ever-difficult question: "Could I sit in tonight?" (Which I realized I didn't really want to do but felt that was what I actually had come there for.) She not only didn't know me, but she had no idea how my singing at her gig might make her look. I might outshine her as a singer, or I might be a tragic joke!

Lavelle wasn't bubbling over with smiles and warmth. She looked at me coolly (she'd seen it all). I was reminded that not everyone is exactly thrilled about my singing career and my needing a break.

She seemed resistant, so I tried my best to be irresistible. "Stacy highly recommended that I come and see you, and that you might like to hear me sing?"

"Did he? I love Stacy, we worked together in the past. Sure, sing something, after the guy does his first song. I'll let him know, he can accompany you."

I chose the song "On Broadway" since it was popular in Paris and easy for the musicians. Unfortunately, I couldn't quite get the groove of it for some reason. I thought, *Who are you, trying to sing this song when it's about a down-and-out guy who plays a guitar and desperately needs a gig in New York?*

Lavelle listened for a few bars. I sensed a lack of interest in her demeanor, but that often happens to "overexposed" singers who become jaded toward anyone they imagine is competition. Next, I sang "Autumn Leaves" in French and English. I started it as a ballad, and then the pianist took it to an upbeat swing. I had wanted it to remain a ballad all the way, but felt he knew better what the room required, so I went along with it.

Lavelle disappeared to join friends, and possibly to observe me from a distance. I had no idea if she was pleased or what. She kept her cards close to her chest. She was a hardworking singer and most likely enjoyed a chance to sit down.

The evening was a turning point in my dislike of the sitting-in experience. I realized that maybe I didn't really have it together to do an amazing rendition of *either* tune with no rehearsal and with musicians I'd never met before. I needed to let the musicians know how I wanted it played, but often that backfired on me, and they overpowered me with their concept of how the music should be delivered. And the songs I chose that night weren't ideal for me to showcase my voice.

I learned that I thrived with familiarity and being well rehearsed. If nothing else, visiting Lavelle at her gig turned out to be an icebreaker into a different music scene and an introduction to these musicians. No one was going to lose their job because I came to Paris! At least, not right away.

15. Getting to Be a Habit with Me

· · · · · · · · · · · · · ·

Every kiss, every hug / Seems to act just like a drug / You're getting to be a habit with me.
— Al Dubin

I WAS NOW A REGULAR CUSTOMER at the Hollywood Savoy and was occasionally filling in for Rochelle. I was performing two sets of jazz tunes as well as a few novelty songs from my repertoire. They needed my, quirky, charismatic talents.

Now that I had proved I had the singing chops and personality, Stacy hired me Thursday nights to give a little extra pizzazz to the Transcontinental Cowboys. They were an American-styled country-and-western band, but never dressed up like cowboys. They were simply underdressed musicians from the States onstage playing music. They covered the classics that audiences loved. They were well rehearsed and tight—a perfect contrast to me; I was bad-assed and loose! A new persona was born onstage the night I showed up wearing my oversized "African queen" wig (as worn by Whitney Houston in *The Bodyguard*) and a cowboy hat, rarely seen in Paris fashion. I called this character "Star Baby of Paris." I sang my country standards: "Great Balls of Fire," "Almost Persuaded," "Stand by Your Man," and "What's New Pussycat?" At the end of every evening, the Sicilian manager, Tony Giangrande, would pay each musician individually in cash "under the table." It was an ideal arrangement that felt secure and sort of loose for both the artists and the proprietor.

I fit right into the eclectic, unconventional crowd of adventuresome, swinging, singing restaurant staff from the States, England, Australia, and Canada. It was like one big unconventional family. Being from funky, unknown Seattle made me appear novel. I decided that if this didn't eventually turn into my gig, it would be a travesty.

I thought about the times in my life when I hadn't fit in. Now I was beginning to feel like I was "in the pocket" with a glamorous conglomerate of quirky talents at a club that was the epitome of "hot cool." I was in my element, aligned with something I wanted.

· · · · · · · · · · · · · · · · ·

Throughout each evening, featured solos were performed by members of the waitstaff, such as the lascivious barroom babe Holly Lane, a former chorus girl who would sing the suggestive "Long John Blues" ("I have a dentist who's over seven feet tall / His name is Doctor Long John") while kicking the highest high-kicks humanly possible. I'm not sure the French people understood the real meaning of that song, but they loved her.

Stacy's direction, with vaudevillian drum rolls from Vic Pitts, made it all work, and the French ate it up.

It was the sultry, featured singer, Rochelle, whose role I could envision myself in. I could really sink my teeth into that. But I couldn't imagine she'd ever give up her gig.

Night after night as master of ceremonies, Stacy kept the show moving. He'd do a short set on the grand piano, warming up the room for Rochelle (in Los Angeles she had been the next-door neighbor to the creators of the Hollywood Savoy, which led to her prestigious role as *la vedette*). The evening ended with the formulaic routine where the waiters and performers gathered onstage, along with some of the tipsy patrons, and together sang (whether we wanted to or not) "Goodnight, Irene," "Amazing Grace," and "Green, Green Grass of Home."

If it was a rousing group of songs, then sometimes he'd include "Battle Hymn of the Republic" as the showstopping climax. Stacy wasn't pleased if someone didn't cooperate with this required "spontaneous" ritual. Sometimes I'd play hooky in the bathroom or blend in with the regulars at the bar. The group finales made me feel overexposed and that it was overkill. I preferred keeping an air of mystery about my availability and mingled with favored patrons, if I could find some. I innately knew I needed downtime to regain my composure and equilibrium. Taking care of yourself is a protective way to keep your act vibrant. Showbiz is not for the faint of heart.

But when I did join in at the end, I couldn't deny it was a great feeling of belonging and the kind of true showbiz camaraderie that I had been missing. It was a frenzied crescendo at the end of the evening! People were hugging, laughing, and dancing. You'd think we were in some hugely successful, long-running, amusing musical variety show—and I guess we were!

16. Madam Lenora

*Pour yourself a drink, put on some lipstick,
and pull yourself together.*
— Liz Taylor

The Savoy was a magnet for colorful characters, including Madam Lenora, the club's infamous cashier. The '60s had been good to her and she remained a throwback to that era, which included her ways of thinking and speaking and the fact that she had rearranged her life by moving to Paris from Southern California and becoming French.

"I've been observing you for the last couple of weeks, Julie, and I'd like to invite you to share my flat, on the Place des Vosges," she said to me one night. "It's an address most people would *kill* for. One bedroom, two baths, I can show it to you tomorrow."

One bedroom? I wondered what this was leading to.

"I'd like to see it," I answered breezily as the band started the intro of my first song. I headed toward the stage in my stretchy pink dress with red heels to the intro of my "Almost Like Being in Love" / "This Can't Be Love" medley. I felt confident, vivacious, and delicious channeling Judy's opening medley at Carnegie Hall. The band was hot with musical magic: Eddy Goldstein on piano, Gus Nemeth on bass, and Vic Pitts of the Harlem Globetrotters' band on drums, all sounding like stallions ready to stampede out of the club. The room was SRO, and the crowd was calling for me! Stacy Macadams yelled out, "Here she is, Julie CascioppO from

Seattle, WashingTON, give it up!"

Madam Lenora was part hypervigilant cashier and part "California Girl," having grown up in Malibu, long-legged, handsome, and Barbie-esque. This particular Amazon wanted me for her roommate, though I wasn't sure what she resonated with in me.

Recently I'd been temporarily camping at my friend Susy's apartment along with a cast of revolving roommates. As I began to get more gigs, I craved a place to call my own to help me flourish. Madam Lenora was an intimidatingly smooth operator with a surprisingly soft heart. Her ten years in Paris had shown her the ropes. And she dressed to the nines in designer remnants from her wealthy marriage. Even at over six feet, she defiantly wore high strappy heels, along with tons of black mascara, which contrasted with her crowning glory: a mane of straight golden hair severely parted down the middle. Her official title was la Caisse (the lady who handles the money). She'd hold court from a high-backed barstool most of the night, sipping champagne while handling transactions with a proprietary air. The place was raking in the francs.

Once I visited her astonishing Place des Vosges apartment, I was sold. The large living room would transform into my bedroom. I vaguely understood Lenora had acquired this beautiful apartment through her French divorce. She only brought up the divorce once, and I sensed I shouldn't pry, since it was definitely not an apartment one came by without sacrifices. It was spacious and sparsely furnished. I would sleep on a "daybed," which was a couch during the day. I had never seen one of those before—where I came from, a bed was a bed and a couch was a couch. Bookcases were built into the walls and a cozy window seat with cushions invited one to take a nap or to gaze out onto the Place des Vosges and dream of duels. A large mirror above the fireplace would be perfect for checking out my look. The building had a lovely courtyard, and the neighboring apartment buildings were similar in structure and well-kept. My new address was 13 rue de Birague, on the Place des Vosges.

It was in the Marais neighborhood near Les Halles, with its eclectic mix of galleries, bistros, and boutiques all mere steps from my front door.

Here I became comfortable with designer shops like Claude Montana, where I found a pair of dramatic ruby-red cat-eye sunglasses, as well as a Jewish delicatessen that was home to my favorite falafel in the city. Now I knew why this was one of the most sought-after addresses in all of Paris; it was *parfait pour moi*.

I sort of missed my family and friends back home but needed to be really far away to shake off their chains I didn't even know held me captive. Living in Paris was a helpful interlude for me to seriously consider the direction my life would take—although frequently it felt like a never-ending party. All I wanted to do was sing, dance, and become famous. Wasn't that what you were supposed to do? I was ready to croon my way through Paris in any underground cave or dark, musty cabaret. To my growing résumé, I added Chez Régine, on the rue Ponthieu; the Jules Verne in the Eiffel Tower; the Hôtel George V; and Le Privilège, in the famous Palace dance club. Paris was a never-ending parade of colorful, haute couture audiences; adulterous lovers; a convention of soccer players from Barcelona; busloads of discombobulated tourists; or simply the boisterous English revelers. I was becoming *la vedette* (a singing star) and Madam Lenora was the older, wiser, established cashier.

I had wondered what living with Madam Lenora would bring. I wasn't sure we'd be compatible. You really don't find out what someone is like, I mean *really like*, until you live with them. Depending on our mood swings, we got along well. We were high-strung individuals living together out of necessity. She liked me and admired my unconventional style. We were an interesting dichotomy.

When you come from a background with a fair amount of chaos and disorder, as I did, you re-create similar dynamics wherever you go—unless you've had lots of therapy. *"No matter where you go, there you are."*

Soon enough, Madam Lenora was reminding me of my mother! But I dismissed the thought from my mind. My mother's unrealistic expectations of "a husband and children" for me caused suffering for both of us. Especially when she repeated, "Give me a grandchild before it's too late!"

Did she think that if she nagged me enough, I'd cave in and give her one? It was unfair of her to ask for that, since she was often absent pursuing her own interests rather than raising us. I'd grown up wild, under the erratic tutelage of my gay older brother, who encouraged me to adopt drag-queen qualities and be outrageous and funny any chance I got. His laughter encouraged me.

I was in Paris to create a healthy distance from my mother and various conventional expectations. Why would I find a roommate with similarities to her? It was uncanny. I was too busy to think about it deeply and not sure it mattered. At least Lenora didn't ask me for a grandchild.

....

The apartment next door to us had been the home of French author and occultist Victor Hugo. From 1853 to 1855, he conducted séances that he claimed connected him with hundreds of spirits including Shakespeare, Aeschylus, Joan of Arc, and Sappho. Now his apartment housed a small, dusty museum, rarely opened to the public.

I'd gaze out the towering windows of the living room, now my bedroom, onto the Place des Vosges where, in past centuries, noblemen fought to the death, dueling with their lethal swords. How could there not be troubled spirits in the surrounding areas, as well as in buildings like ours?

I noticed my new roommate sometimes taking on the ditzy, nonthreatening persona of a spaced-out, fun-loving flower child. In reality she was a sharp cookie, aware of every angle. She knew how to manage everyone, including me, and I was at a place in my life where I felt generous enough to ignore her—like I tried to ignore and avoid my mother both as a child and as an adult. It was a form of self-protection and survival.

One night, half asleep, I actually thought I saw a ghost pacing around my room. But as I awoke, I saw it was Madam Lenora, looking for something she was positive she left in my room. (Everyone had to go through my room to get to the kitchen!)

At times it seemed possible our apartment was inhabited by spirits. Our lights went out regularly, and then magically came on again, as if to tease us. This was never questioned or repaired. We accepted that since we were next door to the Victor Hugo museum and Mr. Hugo had been fond of the occult, of course we'd hear sporadic knockings on our connecting walls and endured flickering lights.

Besides strange sound effects in the night, and the odd assortment of friends both Madam Lenora and I acquired, anything was possible.

Without compunction, she'd eat everything in the fridge and never replace it. One morning I inquired about my peaches, which seemed to have disappeared. Madam Lenora, still wearing last night's makeup, claimed implausibly, while lighting a cigarette, "I got really hungry in the middle of the night, and I knew if I didn't eat just about everything I found, I would have become sick to my stomach! And I knew you wouldn't want me to end up in the hospital. I feel terrible about it, but I guess I'm just that way."

It was confusing to live with someone who was a glamorous, efficient babe at work, yet at home reminded me of an overcaffeinated Raggedy Ann doll. I just wished she could have been the average expat American who knows the importance of grocery shopping. Lenora's domestic skills stopped at coffee and cigarettes.

On my nights off, I sometimes had small dinner parties with friends like Susy, from the Hollywood Savoy, and Ali, a Tunisian concierge at a hotel in the Latin Quarter where Nina Simone was living at the time. He loved to share gossip about Miss Simone, such as when she kept an admirer waiting for eight hours in the lobby and then made a grand entrance completely nude. Ah, to simply go insane in Paris after an extraordinary career!

Madam Lenora was proud of having friends in the French chapter of the Hells Angels. (And who wouldn't be?) They were infamous in the States for crime, manslaughter, and being a public nuisance from driving boisterous motorcycles. But in Paris they seemed pale in comparison, almost sweet and dopey, despite their sweaty and questionable wardrobe choices: leather chaps, dirty kerchiefs, and bulky leather jackets. Their reputation for being petty criminals and wanted by the police preceded them. Occasionally, Madam Lenora would invite them over for a late-night party in our apartment. I fit right in, since it was taking place in my bedroom. There was something more innocent than dodgy about these Hells Angels. I've said it before and I'll say it again: French people are *genteel*—including *les clochards* (the street beggars) and the pickpockets working the crowds in the metro.

My bedroom was the official living room, and if the party went too late, she'd take it into her bedroom so I could sleep (so thoughtful of her).

Madam Lenora had a semi-famous boyfriend, Jean Louis, who sang rock and roll. He was shy, mousy, and slight of build, until he started singing, and then he sounded remarkably like Elvis at the bottom of a hollow well. He'd insist on having the reverb turned up all the way on his microphone, which magically turned him into the "King." The Hells Angels were his bodyguards. When he sometimes spent the night with Madam Lenora, through the thin walls I thought I could hear animals rumbling about, jumping on the bed, and horses neighing.

One night at the Savoy, as I was leaving the stage for intermission, a group of Hells Angels appeared near the entrance—which was unusual. I recognized one of them from the recent house party as he approached me and abruptly lifted me into his arms! Holding me like a baby, he yelled out for the whole club to hear, "She not only sings good—she smells good too!" The audience roared.

I was startled, but one can't help appreciating someone who says such endearing things. It was one of those stellar moments at the Hollywood Savoy. I found myself enjoying the combination of fear and laughter, a remnant from my childhood. More broadly, though, Paris often reminded me of the childhood I wished I'd had—full of fun, beautiful parks, and pretty toys. And I, the darling of all the boys.

Living with my roommate's eccentricities was challenging, but fortunately she was gone most of the time. At first I thought she was unique and unpredictable, never a dull moment. Temporarily it would have been easy to take, but I was hoping this living arrangement could last for a year.

We borrowed clothes from each other, which enabled me to wear some chic designer clothing she'd collected during her married life in Paris. Before the two children and the French ex-husband, I'd heard she'd had a stretch at modeling!

One night before heading off to the club, as we were doing our nails together at the round oak table in the kitchen, she offered me a cigarette and an amphetamine as if it were a snazzy new kind of breath mint.

"By the time we finish smoking our cigarettes," she purred, "our nails will be dry, and we can share a taxi to work."

Once the pill kicked in, I felt euphoric—as if I'd finally found my real mother or best friend or at least a reliable drug connection.

That night I sang with wild abandon. I felt like I owned the stage. I was on fire.

During the intermission, zealous customers, picking up on this mania, offered me champagne, which I drank copiously, just to calm down. Now I understood why some singers are such over-the-top great performers: it's drug and alcohol induced! Not always, but more often than one imagines.

I didn't want to become a statistic. I had the genetic disposition to take drinking further than was good for me. On that night and others, I ignored this nagging notion in the forefront of my mind and imbibed more than I needed. Occasionally I thought, *Maybe I better clean up my act a bit?*

Eventually, though, my drinking while performing was pointed out to me. And hearing that from the right person made it stick.

17. Tor Comes to Visit, Uh-Oh

*One must have chaos in oneself to be able
to give birth to a dancing star.*
— Friedrich Nietzsche

WITH A GLAMOROUS APARTMENT on the Place des Vosges, I thought it might be a good time for Tor to visit me in Paris, since the whole trip had been his idea.

Tor arrived in mid-December for the holidays. Having a boyfriend would alter my style and change people's idea of the woman I wanted them to think I was. I came across as a devil-may-care jazz singer and appeared to be single, although there was someone devotedly waiting in the wings, in Seattle. As I became more comfortable in and knowledgeable about Paris, I was behaving like the most engaging babe in town. Madam Lenora was oblivious to my dilemma.

Tor and I had made plans to travel to Italy and Amsterdam. I could fashionably disappear from Paris and not have to explain all my colorful new friends and flirtations to Tor. He got to meet selected ones, though, like Susie—who was shocked at how subdued I became when Tor was around. Later she told me, "My gawd, Julie, you're like night and day. So demure around him!"

Susie's friend Nancy confided, "Julie, as a couple you don't seem compatible! You could find someone more up your alley."

These comments did not align well with my new paradigm as the jazziest, swingiest singer in Paris, and I felt on some level maybe I wasn't being authentic. But in Paris reinvention was in the air.

It was true, what my friends said: I had to turn down my generator when I was with Tor. I saw him as an authoritarian and father figure. I am not sure how that dynamic came to be, but I participated in creating it. At the time, I didn't have the self-awareness to see how it was damaging to both of us.

One evening, Tor was in the audience at the Hollywood Savoy, watching my act like a hawk—a proud hawk, I thought. Afterward, in private he surprised me by saying, "It was obvious you'd been drinking. You lose your edge and it's noticeable."

I was shocked and didn't like hearing that, especially from him—but I needed to. I looked up to Tor and wanted him to continue to hold me on that pedestal I'd been relaxing on for the first two years of our relationship. But having no one to answer to while in Paris, I could have continued in this insidious behavior and then fallen into the trap of thinking, *No one notices I am tipsy.* I certainly didn't!

Everyone I knew accepted that drinking was part of the territory. And I was grateful to have heard that criticism from Tor, rather than anyone else.

My career and life in Paris seemed to be coming together, but I felt impatient with Tor, even though he was partially supplementing and enabling my experience. Living in Paris had opened up a freer, more exciting way of life—thanks to him. Life with Tor in Seattle *paled* in comparison: his shyness around others, and his bossiness with me, felt . . . oppressive.

He generously took me shopping, and I was making up for lost time. I was ready to spend as much as he'd allow. There were so many tempting baubles and finery, lovely things I'd had my eye on. Like a beautiful knit red dress that I couldn't afford on my own. He commented about my manic purchases and that he felt like shopping was more important than his visit. I explained how I was trying to make it on my own and stay on an honest budget. Now that he was in town, though, all restraint broke loose. He seemed to accept my response.

He offered to purchase a pied-à-terre, *a small apartment of my own* in Paris—in fact, the one I'd been staying in earlier near the Sacré-Coeur! In that moment, I thought, *I don't want to be burdened with owning an apartment.* I knew that my life could go in any direction, and I hoped it would go higher and higher. I believed I needed to be *free* of anything tying me down for successful things to transpire. Idealistically, I believed I had the "stuff" to be a huge success.

It seemed important to be unencumbered. Looking back on it, maybe I shouldn't have turned that down. I wanted everything on *my terms*, and I thought I was a lot more powerful than I was. But the truth was I was powerful *with Tor's assistance*. More than anything, I wanted to steer my own course. But honestly, did I even have a clue?

Since Tor's arrival, I had arranged time off and we planned a few trips. After Italy and Amsterdam, we would return to Paris; then, for Christmas Eve, a trip to Norway to meet his relatives. Norway: a country I had longed to visit more than any in the world! My Norwegian grandmother had filled my imagination with colorful fantasies of the land of majestic fjords, mountain peaks, and fertile valleys.

I'd finally experience the Norwegian Christmas of my grandmother's stories, with all its holiday magic, including a smorgasbord, cross-country skiing, roasted spareribs, pickled herring, and the Christmas Eve special rømmegrøt, a Norwegian sour cream and heavy cream porridge served mainly on high holidays. It would be a Scandinavia-ganza. I imagined that, through all the festivities and viewing the aurora borealis together on snowshoes in the middle of the desolate Norwegian tundra, we would come to know we were meant for each other. The distractions of Paris would conveniently fade and we'd see a path forward for our future.

Although we lived together in Seattle, our relationship was undefined, especially once I went to Paris. Now that we were staying together at Madam Lenora's, Tor brought it up again at the breakfast table, revealing his heart to me: "Julie, once you left Seattle. I fell in love with you again. I've been hoping you'd like to get married? If so, I'm going to go get a real engagement ring."

"Well, right now, my singing career is taking off. I'm not sure I can do both. What's the rush?" His efforts to control me made me feel trapped. "Why do we have to make it official? This is the '80s, marriage is not that necessary anymore."

I had witnessed too many divorces and broken hearts in my short life—particularly those of my parents.

· · · · · · · · · · · · · · · · ·

Our holidays through Rome, Florence, and Amsterdam were an opportunity to readjust to each other, away from Paris and my obsession with my career. Things had smoothed out as we enjoyed all the new sights and sounds and seeing friends we knew in Florence.

Back in Paris, after living semi-single those first months there, I now fell into the role of being Tor's girlfriend again. Recalling his endless fishing trips to Alaska and all the challenges that the long separations put on our relationship, I wasn't sure what I thought.

That particular night in Paris, I had my Savoy gig, and he planned to stay home, maybe even go to bed early. This freed me up to perform the way I was most used to: lively, outrageous, and a little risqué. Maybe I'd even have some champagne.

For my return engagement, I was debuting the curve-accentuating red dress Tor had purchased for me, with a revealing décolletage. Tor had even helped me write a few songs that were funny and sexy. I was winding up the set with one of them.

"I'm a multi-man woman, no one man keeps me satisfied. One guy tried it, and he thanked Jesus when he died."

I had that crowd in the palm of my hand, and the song went through the roof on the climactic ending. I surrendered to the adulation. This was my tribe. I stepped off the stage to rowdy applause, warm drunken smiles, and those friendly pretend kisses!

In the midst of this euphoria, I noticed a ruckus at the main door of the club. The person entering was not part of the usual ambience, but an intruder into my sacred circus. Tor!

He had rifled through my bureau drawers (the sign of a fervent lover?) and found my small red diary recounting the visit of a Swedish playboy who had swept through Paris and caught my eye. I admitted in my journal that he spent the night (which didn't necessarily imply a romantic interlude in Paris at that time).

Full of frustrated passion, imagining scenarios that were much worse or better than what actually happened, Tor went berserk. He stormed into the Hollywood Savoy decimating the hip, jovial vibe I had created!

His wild eyes betrayed the embarrassment of his rage. I had never seen him so out of control. I had just finished my last song of the set and greeted him.

"Tor, what's the matter?" I asked, hoping it had nothing to do with me.

He grabbed the little diary, opened it to the exact page, and handed it to me. "You slept with another man!" he snapped.

"What are you talking about? I never sleep with anyone."

(Gentle reader, out of discretion I'll spare you the details of what actually transpired, because it was of no lasting significance.)

As I glanced at the small book in his hand, I saw my writing. I had almost forgotten that experience. For some reason, I did not react with outrage at him for having gone through my private dresser, searching and finding God knows what.

"He was *gay*, and he stayed late at our party—until he passed out!" (I hoped it sounded plausible.) Tor wasn't having it. Steam emanated from his face! I'd never experienced this level of passion aimed at me before.

Embarrassed to be creating a scene, I directed him to follow me downstairs: "Let's chat privately instead of being the floor show!"

"Here, read it!" he said. I couldn't say much in my defense as I took the diary into my hands, a tiny book meant for jotting down fragmented moments to remember, for no one's eyes but mine. I was grateful that I'd been a discreet journalist and hadn't filled the diary with sordid details! But from the way he was acting, maybe I had written more than I should have?

I couldn't concentrate on reading the diary, as I was suddenly aware that I might be in harm's way, and he might be capable of a crime of passion. (Which was legal in Paris.)

I had never seen him so tormented. It was scary. I repeated with emphasis, "He was simply a gay friend and I was telling him about you!" I feebly continued, "Madam Lenora had a late-night party with the Hells Angels." (Always implicate others when too much heat is on you.) "And the Swede tagged along and stayed the night because he was too drunk to even go back to his hotel."

I reinforced my original defense: "HE WAS A HOMOSEXUAL ALCOHOLIC FROM STOCKHOLM!" I was hoping this was softening the blow while making a point.

Meanwhile, Savoy patrons were coming downstairs to use the restrooms and curiously glancing our way, wanting to hear what this fight was about. Tor was pacing in the small hallway, noticeably distressed, unglued, and this was coming from an undiscoverable place in his tortured soul that was painful to be witnessing. Did this mean that my living a carefree life in Paris was igniting a powder keg of excruciating emotion in someone I cared about? Was I that oblivious?

I hadn't been in this kind of trouble before, and I didn't like it. I couldn't find my center of gravity. Some immense force was trying to squish me down, metaphorically speaking, and I refused to let it happen. I had never been so pointedly accused, so terribly guilty, and so frantic in trying to find a convincing explanation.

At one point, his anger erupted from his primal depths as he raged: "I can't believe you slept with a *Swede!*"

So, *that* was it . . .

"I did *not* sleep with him!" I gasped, as if my life depended on it. Because in a way, I believed that if I lost this fight with Tor, I would be lost for the rest of my life. I added, "He wouldn't even want to sleep with me—*he's gay.*"

Oops, was that a valid reason to not sleep with someone? I was growing tired of this quarrel. During times of volatility it seemed I said anything that popped into my head. I realized I didn't even believe myself. I was beginning to think that I didn't belong in a monogamous relationship because I didn't have the confidence to be honest.

Embarrassed, and not wanting to be the one responsible for this scene, I encouraged him to return to the apartment. I had one more set to perform that night.

Tor's greatest fears had been triggered: that I would find another man, in the most romantic city in the world, but I really hadn't.

Later on, at the apartment, after a long night of explaining, denying, and crying, we made some kind of peace that helped us get through the night.

The next morning, I awoke, not sure what or where I was. Oh, yes, my apartment on the Place des Vosges. Tor was not next to me. He had been up for hours, dressed and packed. He had changed his ticket to Norway on the telephone in Madam Lenora's room and was leaving immediately without me. (She hadn't come home the night before, thank God.)

He planned on leaving with my most prized possession—a radio / tape recorder—that he had brought me from Seattle. As much as I had wanted to be with him in Norway, I accepted that if he didn't want me to join him there, I could survive in Paris. But please, no—whatever you do—*don't* take my tape recorder console! It was a crucial piece of equipment, which for some reason was impossible to find in Paris. I needed it more than anything to work as a singer. I traded him the treasured orange-juice squeezer, which we both cherished. It had been one of my many thoughtful Christmas presents from him.

We hugged, formally, and he left for Norway, leaving me behind. It felt as though we'd broken up. I could not accept it. I planned to change his mind.

I was alone now to sort my emotions and face the music, or lack thereof, for the holidays. It began snowing, delicately, then heavily, and by the time Tor's flight left for Oslo, Paris was transformed into a white, deathlike dream. Its crystalline beauty was juxtaposed with my needling depression. What would happen next?

Tor had anchored me in place, and now I was loose: a ship without a captain. Could I manage without him in the wings? Did I want that? Being untethered felt frightening. I was abandoned, haunted with guilt and paralyzing ennui.

Luckily, as the ensuing days unfolded, I had my friends Susie and Nancy for comradery and nights on the town, including dancing at the Palace, where the two of them arranged to have handsome guys dance with me.

Many long-distance phone calls to Norway and letters to Seattle let Tor know how deeply I loved him. I promised him I'd return in the spring and we could attempt to start over.

Me as a young child with my mother and brothers Norman, Tony and Danny

My parents, Solveig and Sam

Young portrait of myself full of dreams

The bon voyage party in Seattle with Jackie Roberts, owner of the Pink Door

Mia Newman, my first friend in Paris

A festive weeknight at the Hollywood Savoy, with Susie Robinson on mic

At the Hollywood Savoy   Rochelle and me at Place Saint-Sulpice

ALL PARIS PHOTOS TAKEN BETWEEN 1983 AND 1990

. . . .

Rue du Dragon /
Jerôme de Zilva Reid,
talented fashion designer
who became my personal
designer
Photos by Jerôme de Zilva Reid

Illustrations by Christian Debarre, a devoted regular at the Hollywood Savoy who grew to be known in France as a "genius comic"

A random man offered to take this photo as I lingered on a quai of the Seine

Photographer Bernard Brezet

Susie Robinson, Sandy-Girl, Claudia Phillips and Madam Lenora, dear friends I met while working at the Hollywood Savoy. Notice the sparkle in my eyes as I speak to the iconic Cary Grant.

Daniel Cueva, artist friend

With Richard Goodwin, famous producer of epic films like *Romeo and Juliet* and *A Passage to India*

Party invitation at Le Palace

Modeling one of Daniel's painted gowns

A faux tiger winter coat I purchased in Paris
Photo by Mike Walker

Decadence and Jacques, good friends who helped pave my way

Nancy Cotton and Susie Robinson

Living on the Place des Vosges with Madam Lenora

The Norwegian twins who got me in touch with my Norwegian roots

Entertaining Parisians with a number of patriotic songs for a Fourth of July expat event

With Stacy Macadams at the Bush-Dukakis election-night party at the American Embassy

Photo shoot in Barcelona, then back to Paris
Photo by Michael McCarthy

Publicity photo from the early 1980s (with hat purchased in Paris)
Photo by Mary Kay Birnet

With Mark Morris at the final party in Brussels

All dolled up in black, with my light-pink feather shoes, for the pipe organ museum gala in Norfolk, UK

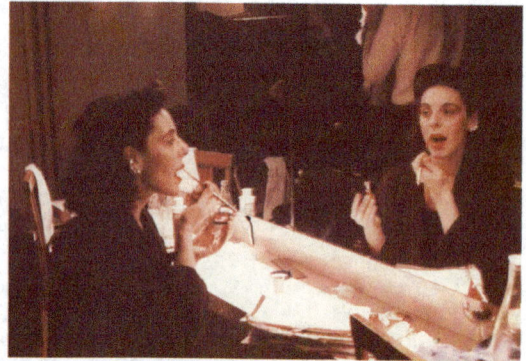

Preparing for my gig in Deauville with the Cowboys

The Cowboys / We never looked more classic than when we performed in Deauville.

With Mark Morris and Linda Dowdell in Brussels

"You made my night!"
—Baryshnikov

18. Flirting with the Famous

* * * * * * * * * * * * * *

*You may wear out your iron-soled shoes searching for
what arrives without effort when the time is right.*
— Chinese proverb

ONE JANUARY EVENING AT THE CLUB, Rochelle surprised me by saying, "I'm so tired of this scene and can't keep doing this." I knew she had issues to focus on, one being her Italian lover.

We were in one of the corner banquettes, chatting more than watching the show. Sipping from her bottle of Evian, without looking up, she asked, "Would you like to take over this gig of mine?"

"I would LOVE it," I answered quickly, never imagining she'd offer such a gift. With the jazz trio already in place and a built-in audience, having a regular gig at the Hollywood Savoy would be perfect and positively life-altering for me. I could focus on developing interesting arrangements, select material that showcased my voice and personality, and create a vibe like I had at the Pink Door in Seattle. Most importantly, I wouldn't have to hit the streets looking for gigs so often. Suddenly there was a good reason to stay in Paris longer.

She glanced up from her mineral water, checking my reaction, and said, "Take it! It's yours," as if relinquishing her unwanted pommes frites. I sat still, immersed in the good feelings of having received the thing I wanted most. It was a dream come true for me, a real break.

Here I had thought we were having a casual conversation, but we were making a life-changing, marvelous deal! Rochelle was calm, cool, collected. Familiar with Hollywood deals. Never getting too worked up about anything. Hollywood royalty had a secret code: "Be cool."

I was furtively out of my mind with utter delight. But I didn't want to seem too excited. Being cool was going to be my new rule. I was afraid she might suddenly change her mind.

Stacy was tickled that I was official now. It looked like I'd be staying indefinitely since I was offered a steady five nights per week! I couldn't wait to let Tor know—he'd be so happy, if he started speaking to me again.

Now I knew what I'd be up to almost every night, and many of my days would be spent partially in rehearsals and gathering material for my performances. My confidence would increase through consistent performing and socializing with attractive audience members. I could chill confidently at the Hollywood Savoy, while being dressed to the nines! *Because this will be My Gig!* I told myself. *I will own this room!*

I was now part of the music scene in one of the most enchanting cities in the world.

Once I was officially accepted by the management, including Stacy (what could they do, Rochelle had fish to fry), I slipped into my groove as easily as flipping pancakes on a well-greased griddle. I was made for this gig. They needed my gutsy, quirky, charismatic talents.

One evening shortly after I had established myself as the jazz diva of the club, the staff was hyper excited because Cary Grant, one of Hollywood's most iconic movie stars, was stopping in Paris on a publicity junket, marketing a new Fabergé perfume! He and his entourage took a circular booth facing the stage and watched the show. At a certain point, the paparazzi invited all the singing waitresses and other performers, including me, to gather round his ringside booth, where he sat with four stunning blonde beauties from the modeling agency. We were asked to strike some poses fawning over him—as if we had to be told to!

He was a famous leading man, and had gotten more attractive with age, as men tend to do in show business.

Overcome with his magnetism, at one point, in the middle of frenetic activity, I boldly asked, "May I have your autograph, Mr. Grant?" He turned his head up at me and said, "I never sign anything anymore!" The crowd chuckled at his clever retort.

I replied, "Well, maybe you'd like mine?" I handed him a signed coaster advertising a popular dish recently put on the menu, "Carpaccio Cascioppo" (thinly sliced, tender, raw meat).

Everyone laughed, including Cary Grant and his entourage. The paparazzi instantly snapped a shot of our interaction. Surrounded by the adoring Sleazettes of the Hollywood Savoy, we all made it into *Star* magazine and onto the cover of *Paris Match*: Susie Robinson, Nancy Cotton, Claudia Phillips, Madam Lenora, and Sandy Girl fresh from Australia.

Meeting famous people and other luminaries at the Hollywood Savoy was de rigueur. One night a rather sedate, older, handsome man was introduced to me.

"Julie, this is Marcello Mastroianni," my colleague said. I thought he looked familiar, but I wasn't quite the Italian film buff that I later became.

He kissed my gloved hand, offering an *"Enchanté, mademoiselle."*

Charmed, I was! But at that time I didn't understand what a famous movie star he was in Europe. He was polite and understated, and I realized that sex appeal transcends age! I still have those black sheer gloves. Since then, I've done my homework studying his films, including Fellini's *La Dolce Vita* and *8½*. Listening to an interview with him and Fellini, I dreamily recalled, *Wow, he kissed my glove—and my hand was in it!*

19. Everything Must Change

What would a woman who truly valued herself do?
— My therapist

Now, in early 1984 in Paris, without Tor, and with our relationship in limbo, I had all winter and till the end of spring to consider my next move. I was now the headliner at the Hollywood Savoy and getting significant, consistent exposure. Performing five nights a week as well as guest appearances at other clubs and gala events kept me out of trouble and happily making money, though never quite enough. The Parisian joie de vivre and SRO crowds encouraged my bold performance style, which included singing original blues and improvising lyrics while interacting with the audience. This formula, partly conceived by Stacy Macadams and which I was now calling the Julie Cascioppo Experience, captured the audience's attention. The Hollywood Savoy was the place to see and be seen.

Benard Ighner, the composer of the award-winning song "Everything Must Change" (one of my favorites), frequented the Hollywood Savoy. Even though it's one of the most perfect songs ever written depicting the simplicity and pathos of life and death, the living composer was discreet about his fame.

He, like many shy artists, found the Savoy a welcoming port in the storm, a place to hang out and check up on the scene.

At first I had no idea who he was; I just saw a Black man with a distingué air about him, with whom I'd occasionally exchange easy, fun repartee while I was on my breaks. One night after I had finished singing that song, he was standing by the bar and greeted me nonchalantly, "I like that song."

I responded graciously, "Thank you!"

He added, dryly, "I wrote it."

Pretending not to be impressed with his admission, I said, "Oh, really? I love that song, it relays deep feeling, and the words are easily embraced."

I meandered off in search of Stacy, to confirm that Benard was indeed telling me the truth.

"Yes," he said, glancing toward the bar "That's Benard Ighner, the composer and lyricist of that wonderful song, and when he sings it, it's mind-blowing. I've known him for years. He's here all the time."

This clarified for me that he was the real deal.

. . . .

The more I performed, the more my dynamic as a singer was beginning to truly find its stride. Audiences and musicians loved the international flavor of swinging to retro jazz standards and love songs, sung in French, Spanish, and Italian—songs like "Bésame Mucho," "What Is This Thing Called Love?" "I Love Paris," "You and the Night and the Music," and "Begin the Beguine" (in Italian). All the important ingredients were in alignment with the muse and planets. My repertoire became my emotional life, which wasn't clicking at the time my career was taking off. I tended to live in fantasy when it came to love.

I felt carefree on this gig because the weight of its success wasn't all on my shoulders. The entertainment there included the talented singing waiters and waitresses, Stacy Macadams performing his Americana set, and then me with a wonderful jazz trio. I could relax, sing, and schmooze, doing only two sets per night (although there is nothing relaxing about entertaining—I had to deliver the goods!).

I'd fashioned an alluring performance that it seemed had broad appeal. I pooled my talents for music, comedy, and theater and shared that mélange with Paris. I loved adding new songs and writing my own. I put together flamboyant getups and enjoyed trusting my innate style both as a performer and as a woman of the world. I was sure I was born to do this. And I was making more money than I'd ever made as a singer.

I felt that I had grown as a performer and it was time for a breakthrough. I longed to become more successful on the stairway to stardom.

Now my desire was to make audio recordings and television appearances, so I could be seen by the quirk-loving Europeans with an appreciation for foreign talent.

Chatting about this topic with Benard Ighner during an intermission, I mentioned my desire to expand my audiences and wondered if I should hire a publicist or something else.

He confided in me that he knew exactly what I needed to do to get to the next level of success. "Don't waste your money, Julie. If you want to get famous in Paris, you need to do your own publicity stunt. Do you want me to tell you what to do?" And he came closer.

"I am all ears!" I was finally having the kind of conversation that I wanted with him. I leaned in, wondering what he might have to say. I also wondered if he might be gay, but that didn't matter. I didn't have to fall in love with everyone who wanted to help me.

He was usually inscrutable, but in this conversation, his head tilting to the side, he seemed to channel ideas from a parallel universe, bestowing them to me as rare gifts. His mischievous, moody eyes, for the first time, twinkled just a bit. "You've got to get a convertible Cadillac and fill it with straw," he murmured. The mention of straw was the first sign of my doubt; I wondered if he was toying with me.

"Then, gather six to eight piglets and have someone drive you up and down the Champs-Élysées while you're holding them and singing over a loudspeaker!"

I let his magic spell be cast, hanging on to each word of his seductive voice and imagining those innocent little pink piggies.

He added, "I promise, it will catapult you to stardom!"

That sounded ludicrous. But I wanted to believe him.

I could pull something like this off in Seattle, for I had a friend in Seattle who collected Cadillacs. But in Paris, I certainly did not yet have the contacts or audacity to gather baby pigs, let alone know anyone with a Cadillac convertible.

To top it off, I wasn't sure if Benard was just pulling my leg. He was the only person I knew who had the pluck to tease me so unkindly. I speculated about his outlandish suggestion and, without ever knowing for sure, let it go as a memorable and hilarious prank at my expense.

I suppose I was asking for that kind of practical joke to be played on me, since my act onstage consisted of a fair amount of teasing and exaggerating to the audiences. Was I getting a little of my own medicine?

But Benard never cracked a smile on that one. In fact, now that I think of it, he rarely smiled.

. . . .

I had the fantasy-laden strategy that if enough people saw me, I could become famous—or at least hugely successful. While performing on Paris stages I noticed that it isn't how many people—it's a question of the right people seeing you and what kind of money they think you can make for them as a commodity. Then there are the fans who feel a deep rapport with you. Through their involvement with you they gain the satisfaction of contributing to your greater success. I hadn't had grand exposure, nor did it look like I was capable of handling it if that did happen. On some level, I was afraid to leave my comfort zone. Paris wasn't a hopped-up, ambitious, life-and-death competitive city, like Los Angeles and New York. Paris suited me and my limitations.

Not to mention all those handsome men lined up at the bar captivated by me!

A close friend revealed to me that, while sitting at the bar, he'd overheard a conversation between two men debating if I were a "female impersonator." In a way, I was. I was becoming known as an audacious, unpredictable performer! Someone sultry, dangerous, and entertaining—

and hey, I might even be a *man*!

Stacy kept a sharp eye on the show with his peripheral vision, sometimes straightening out the mic cord so I could move freely, while he yelled above the music, "Here she comes! Work the crowd, Jewel!"

I had no idea what he meant or what I was specifically doing, but I kept the crowds laughing and mesmerized with excitement. Gradually I realized what that expression "work the crowd" meant: connecting with an audience and being comfortable with that power.

Coming offstage, I'd be surrounded by fawning fans, admiring my accoutrements, wanting to touch my accessories to absorb the "magic." "Don't touch the art!" I'd say playfully as they took my hand to admire the baubles. French women stick to the adage that "less is more," but seeing me all jeweled up, they were fascinated as well. I could feel that this singing engagement was taking me places, though I didn't know where. I cinched my belt and held on for the ride.

There was always someone reminding me of my contribution to the Paris landscape.

20. Cocktail Party with a Famous Jazz Cat

. . . .

A girl should be two things: classy and fabulous.
— Coco Chanel

O NE OF THE PERKS OF HAVING A CONSISTENT GIG at a club is that some nights there's a special event when your musical services are required for only one set. Then you get off early and you're dressed for Paris.

With no particular plans, the musicians—including my favorite sidekick, pianist Eddy Goldstein—and I found ourselves invited to a party, impromptu. Since it was near the Place des Vosges, I thought, *Pourquoi pas?* (Why not?) *Allons-y.* (Let's go.)

It was the kind of gathering where, the minute you walked in, you felt "electricity." It didn't matter who you were with—everyone was blending with one another and was vivacious, exciting, and possibly in an altered state. It was a *fête*, like a celebration in Paris should be: artists, expats, drunken diplomats, African embassy characters—you know, the kind of partygoers who knew how and when to cut loose. The guests were talking at a fevered pitch. You had to be in the right mood for it, and I certainly was. I felt especially energetic, I was dressed to perform, and the night was young.

Who knows what enchantment was brewing that evening? It was a thrill to be a part of it. I felt in sync with the spirits of the night. People were drinking whiskey and gin and all kinds of delicious French wine and sampling an assortment of tantalizing tidbits. Someone was having a fantastic party. I had no idea who was the host.

I felt sultry in one of my retro cocktail dresses. I was beginning to get the hang of always looking good anywhere I went in Paris. I noticed that the better I looked, the more fun I had. When I look good, I *feel* good—and it translates in any language!

"If you can't go BIG, stay home," my friend Shannon Piper used to say.

Sometimes, I forgot that I wasn't onstage. Actually, Paris was my stage, and a party in Paris was exciting theater.

While at this party, I easily retained my amped-up performance personality: outgoing, confident, and high-spirited like I was onstage—but this was real life. I liked it when the two faces of Julie were in sync.

I was introduced to a famous sax player known as a "genius" in the jazz world, who was currently gigging in Europe. We fell into an involved flirtatious repartee. I can't remember the details, but it was an improvisational chat: deep, funny, and intelligent! And it was enough to make me feel he was interested. (Maybe his secret was that he made everyone feel interesting.)

We had a dose of extraordinary fun talking and laughing. Then, in the middle of a great guffaw, he exclaimed, "They don't make women like you anymore." Now that was a refreshing phrase to hear from a man's lips!

The party continued as we kept laughing and talking. Someone was smoking marijuana nearby and I think we were getting a contact high. In fact, we took a few puffs.

At a certain point, it was time for me to leave. Eddy wanted to stay at the party with his cronies. As I gathered myself together, my new friend joined me, and we walked out together. He offered to see me home safely. Walking in Paris was inviting in most neighborhoods, as they were well lit and designed for it.

As we walked along the street, the sky had an uncanny stillness after the intensity of the party. There was an unforgettable feeling in the cool night breeze, as if we were on our way to falling in love. The moonlight peeping through the clouds guided our stroll, possibly wondering what potential this synchronistic meeting of two strangers held.

Lingering at the Gothic gate into the courtyard of my apartment building on Place des Vosges, he said, "I really want to come in."

I replied coyly, "Not tonight." (That was a line Eddy Goldstein had taught me in order to find out if a man is seriously interested. Eddy knew all the moves in the dance of romance. He'd followed a French woman to Paris, and almost died of a broken heart when it fizzled.) Plus, I was not exactly single myself. Tor remained an important character in my destiny and I was hoping to repair that snag when I returned to Seattle in late spring.

But the sax player stated emphatically, "This is our only chance!"

"Why is that?" I asked.

"My wife is out of town for the weekend."

Wife?! Chance? I pondered. I had a habit of forgetting to bring up the question "Are you by any chance married?" Since I wasn't, I naively assumed no one else was. (Who'd want to be married in Paris?) I had to remember to ask because French men had a very available way of acting with strangers, although this musician was American. One normally assumed someone was single if they were coming on to you. But, I learned more than once, that wasn't the case in Paris.

I was fascinated by his guileless audacity, as if he were casually announcing that "the milkman won't deliver on Sunday, so I'll have to stop at the market and grab some." And it always amazed me that a man would think a woman would want to do that, without at least a few dates, dinner, and flowers!

Alcohol played a fundamental role when it did happen, which was rare, but occasionally—at that time in my charmed life—it crossed my mind.

Did he have *no* morals? Or did he just drop them somewhere at the Gare du Nord? Did he think I had nothing better to do? (I didn't, but what a nerve to ask for a one-night stand—and especially with a kind of woman "they don't make anymore."

He was an elite jazz star, and in the big picture, I was an aspiring singer. He probably thought that we were a dreamy combination, *that had a chance of working out to his benefit!* Maybe he'd share some tips about singing, or circular breathing?

What was in it for me? I wanted someone pivotal and devoted. Long-term love: three weeks at least! Besides, it would be too much work to start off a relationship by breaking up a marriage.

Did we even have anything in common besides music? He was a dynamic horn player (and horns usually got in my way, tooting away when I wanted to be singing). I was sensitive and marginally neurotic—that's why I was in Paris! I wasn't sure when Tor might resurface. Since his return to Seattle I'd heard from people that he looked like he'd been in a Parisian prison camp and seemed lost without me. I had promised to come home at some point. I just couldn't say . . . precisely when.

The saxplayer's words "They don't make women like you anymore" echoed reassuringly in my memory. I wondered what he meant by that. (I'll just make something fantastic up!)

In the end, he took no for an answer. I guessed that having a pleasant flirtation with a jazz genius felt better than a lifetime of regret over an unrealistic liaison.

21. Decadence

Rooted in the world but reaching for the stars.
— Unknown

Even though gainfully employed as a singer at the Hollywood Savoy, I still felt compelled to find variety in exposure. I believed my willingness to croon at any venue that said yes was my golden key to opportunity in Paris. This seemed to strengthen my international cachet and reaffirm my having something of value to offer the world.

I accepted an engagement at a club called l'Opéra, an early gig I could complete before my Savoy shows. They wanted "jazz," a word that had different meanings in Paris, which worked to my advantage. I was singing lounge and cabaret songs and just called it jazz, as everyone else was singing anything they wanted that wasn't classical and it seemed to fit under the umbrella of jazz.

Located across the street from the actual Paris Opéra, the club had beckoned me with its flashing neon lights offering "Live Jazz" when I'd visited the American Express office to cash my dwindling traveler's checks. It had an iconic address and a catchy name, but it seemed to have an identity crisis and was in need of cachet.

The club's interior was the wrong kind of lavish, overdecorated with chrome and red velvet. Colossal photographs of Josephine Baker, Jean Harlow, Humphrey Bogart, and Clark Gable dwarfed the room and made one feel minuscule.

Wall-to-wall mirrors meant that no matter where you looked you saw your reflection, which wasn't always comforting. Too many mirrors can be disturbing. ("Who's that woman looking at me? She looks like me! Oh my God, it's me!")

Besides its prime location near the metro and taxi stands, l'Opéra had all the possible pizzazz to make its *club de jazz* a hit in Paris, or it should have been, but there wasn't much action during aperitif hour, when I performed.

The owners were an ominously formal yet handsome pair emanating a dark vibe. They reeked of tension, suspicious of anyone entering their too-precious premises, yet they hired me to sing. My predecessor, a petite, athletic Algerian woman, was angrily gathering her sound system as I was leaving. I asked her if she was a singer.

She snapped, "I don't sing *here* anymore!"

Whew, that was good news. She made me nervous.

She revealed that she was the fastest singer in Paris and had many other gigs. I was impressed. I had never heard that being the "fastest singer" anywhere was a quality to aspire to. I knew that wasn't me; I liked to spend time with the lyrics, enunciating and making sure my audience understood exactly what I was singing about.

At that time, I wanted singing gigs and thought quantity, not quality. The female owner's penetrating eyes accused me of some offense I couldn't recall; perhaps it was that her husband had hired me without consulting her. He reminded me of Napoleon with his barrel chest and dashing eyebrows over rapidly darting eyes. They would have been well cast in a *Twilight Zone* episode.

Although she was a beauty, her dour face portended trouble in paradise. Her makeup appeared professionally overdone, and the expensive jewelry she wore revealed that she was in charge. I observed, at the end of my shift when she paid me, that she handled the francs like a pro, despite her beautifully long, manicured nails. Was this couple ahead of the curve—or behind the eight ball? I sensed that they didn't know how to take me, and I didn't know how to be with them.

The anxiety and nervous sweat emanating from the pores of this establishment made me uneasy, like something terrible might happen any moment. I figured I might not last too long here myself.

Running from one gig to another on the same night gave me a feeling of "success." (I figured the more I performed the better I'd get. But I'm not really sure that's how it works.) At first I felt self-conscious bustling down the boulevards in my theatrical performance drag, hailing taxis off the bustling Avenue de l'Opéra before and after the gig, but I eventually grew comfortable accepting that I was now simply part of the city's exquisite decor. In Paris, a woman dressed like me was not too unusual.

That first night, my opening song was "Hit the Road Jack," which I sang with total conviction, possibly as a caution to myself, with Eddy Goldstein on piano following my cues to "take it to the max." The high-powered spotlights blinked off and on dramatically with blinding force, perhaps to inspire a disco number, which wasn't in my repertoire at the moment. I was singing "retro jazz" before Diana Krall made it into the next fashionable big thing.

Abruptly, the lights went dark, and one tiny spotlight shone in the far corner of the stage, while I was in the center. Who was running the lights?

I gradually figured out that the reason for the complicated vibe about l'Opéra was that at 10 p.m. each evening it morphed into an elite, semiprivate after-hours operation called Le Club de l'Opéra and remained open till 4 a.m. They altered the name to distinguish the real attraction—a flashy, splashy DJ with a silver sound system who arrived each night by limousine.

VIP members each maintained a personal stash of alcohol above the bar, for everyone to see—with their name emblazoned on it!

I never hung out to see what the late-night scene might be, as I was headlining back at the Hollywood Savoy (all warmed up and ready to face a more hospitable club scene), where I was the star attraction and the audience knew it.

The following day, in Cinderella fashion, l'Opéra reverted to being simply a bar where I sang for a few unhappy happy hours. I wondered why the audiences seemed unsophisticated, humorless, and almost anti-American. Was it me? Or perhaps because there were no gay men in the audience?

One early evening while singing my showstopping opening number in Italian, "Begin the Beguine" (a clever choice, had I been singing in Rome), I noticed two people in the audience paying attention. They were a healthy-looking strawberry blonde who looked fresh out of New Jersey and her swarthy companion. She wore an impossible amount of extra-glossy fuchsia lipstick that, on a stage, would alone mesmerize an audience. (I've always said "Lipstick brings life"; I made a mental note to ask her where she got it.) She wore one dangling earring hanging down into the middle of her forehead, as did some exotic Arabic women. She smiled warmly as she leaned into the slight, dark-haired man smoking a hookah pipe. I thought to myself, *He's wearing Armani, and she looks like an extra from Cher's "Gypsies, Tramps and Thieves" video. Another Russian hooker out with a john.*

Directing my attention toward this unlikely couple, I began to sing Sonny and Cher's "Baby Don't Go." The lively lyric perked her up. I could tell by the sparkle of her half-full champagne glass and joyful gyrations that we had a lot in common.

During my break, I introduced myself and learned she was from New Hampshire, across the country from Seattle. I'd never met anyone from there.

Confidently, she declared, "I'm Decadence!"

I responded, "I am too, but what's your name?"

"A long time ago it was Linda!"

We burst into laughter and our friendship was born in that instant. Wow, she understood my humor and didn't take it personally—a lovely quality that I wish more people had.

Her strong, feminine voice was full of feeling. I imagined she had robust vocal cords, like a Jack LaLanne Glamour Stretcher! Her tone, "placed" deep behind her nose, emitted a warm, subterranean, nasal resonance, reminding me somewhat of a foghorn, but in a good way. (Distinct voices activated my fascination with vocal coaching in Paris.)

She was a singer as well. Here was someone close in age to me, who dines out with unlikely men, and struggles, I assumed, to survive in Paris and get a break as a singer. We had things in common! She was a rock singer and wrote her own material, while I sang whatever spoke to me, written by great songwriters.

Over time Decadence slowly became my confidante. I had friends from other countries, but I felt a camaraderie with her because she, like me, believed she wanted and needed to become a star, but most likely would never be. But with a name like Decadence, how could it not happen?

She worked as an au pair. To me, that would be the worst kind of entanglement—to find yourself taking care of someone's children when you wanted to pursue your own calling. I chose not to have children in order to have a career.

She shared terrible stories of the French family she worked for taking advantage of her. Besides childcare, she did chores, took the madam's verbal abuse, and lived in a small room at the top of their apartment, the *chambre de bonne* (maid's quarters). Decadence appeared to have no choice. This was how she was able to live in Paris. We exchanged phone numbers and had long, deep conversations into the night. She was someone I could share my deepest concerns with, and knowing she was listening made my various concerns less worrisome.

I introduced her to my friends at the Hollywood Savoy—Susie, Stacy, and Eddy Goldstein—and invited her to sing for a real audience. She insisted she knew the famous "Summertime" from Porgy and Bess. Yet onstage, she had no idea what key she might sing it in, let alone the lyrics. She was too unique and "out there" for my crowd. But I loved to include the excluded. For example, I invited her to an upcoming paparazzi party where she could meet a few of my French friends, celebrities, and fans. The moment Decadence arrived, I noticed, as did all present in the room. I was chatting with two French reporters, one from *60 Minutes* and the other from the *Hollywood Reporter*, as she swooshed through the room, wearing some kind of lace tablecloth as a poncho, black-and-white horizontally striped tights, and fringed cowboy booties decorated with various chains. One reporter mumbled, "Halloween?" The other laughed and said, "Mama Cass!"

The guys chuckled as if they had a right to critique her, not realizing that she was one of my closest friends and knew secrets of my life. (And by the way, Mama Cass was a famous star!) Their comments were somewhat amusing, but I had lost interest in talking to them. When Decadence asked for directions to the bathroom, my friend Benoit cringed and said he imagined she was quite "diseased." I was shocked that people were so judgmental. In the beginning, I had also been skeptical of her unique way of dressing, but she wasn't shabby. Her style was eclectic; she complemented her thrift-store finds with layers of flea-market jewelry, and her pretty, cherubic face was always dramatically made up. She was preparing to be a rock singer; give the girl a break, you slobs!

Decadence's singing voice had soul and resonance, but she struggled to stay on pitch. But, oh, how she tried. It almost didn't matter that she couldn't sing because her songs were atonal. No one in my circle followed avant-garde rock music at that time. She didn't have any gigs because she was busy juggling the Frenchwoman's kids and practicing her music. She might have flourished in New York.

She also had an inexplicable affinity for North African men, as they did her. And at one time she lived in a colorful arrondissement where their culture was accepted with exotic markets, tea shops, and smoky cafés that most people of Paris shunned.

I got emotional support during our phone chats, something I didn't know I needed. She was like a warm blanket of understanding and humorous insight. Above all, she had empathic qualities with a disarming amount of deep spiritual knowledge. We shared our dramas, traumas, and hopes. She understood what I was going through. Since my falling-out with Tor, I was slowly, painfully trying to decide what to do with my life.

"Do you think I should go home and marry Tor and let this be enough, or remain in Paris and find my way, without my safety net?"

"Julie, you are so talented and amazing, you'll be fine no matter what you do."

I wished I could believe her. I couldn't understand why I doubted myself so deeply, and why was I spending so much time in Paris. Was I afraid to be honest with myself and return to the life I left behind? On the other hand, why couldn't I cut those ties and commit to succeeding in Paris?

Decadence had something I hadn't often found in other friends: she listened deeply, honestly, and with a nonjudgmental heart. We were pals, wandering through Parisian thrift shops and frequenting Arab neighborhoods where people seemed to know her and say hello. She had an excellent eye for finding unusual, bold costume jewelry or cheap treasures at the small Arab stores. She showed me how to barter with flea-market sellers: "Julie, you gotta be willing to walk away and act like you really don't want it." She thrived in that milieu.

It was fun to hang out with someone who had her sense of adventure. She was observant and intelligent, and she found me hilarious! Her warm friendship was an affirmation I deeply appreciated.

She believed that she might be channeling Janis Joplin. I thought she was quite eccentric, but aren't we all? I listened to her strange beliefs, as I was very much like her, but not quite so close to the edge of no return.

Decadence shared that she had been assaulted more than a few times when she was unemployed in Paris, sleeping in parks with her most prized possession, her guitar, locked between her legs to keep it safe. She confided that there was a reason for holding her guitar so preciously: "Some creepy dudes stole my guitar while I was sleeping in a park."

I replied, "Sleeping alone in a park? That's like something I would never, ever do! Then what happened?" It felt like prying to ask.

"I chased them down the street screaming, 'I'll die without my guitar. Give it back.'"

I could imagine how dramatically she had to beg. They agreed; then they assaulted her but let her keep her guitar. (How generous.)

It was uncomfortable hearing her stories about living on the street—both riveting and repulsive. Even with her strong bravado, she seemed easily victimized. And as with so many people I met in Paris, I was never sure if their stories were true. I stood on a precipice and suspended my disbelief, listening between the lines. In any case, I enjoyed her friendship and admired her courage to live dangerously—something I did not care to do, ever.

I was mesmerized by her stories. Her speech, animated by that shocking fuchsia lipstick, remained compelling. We had a compassionate friendship despite all the differences between us. When I spoke of my conflicted situation, regarding remaining in Paris or going home, she was on my side. She stuck up for me in every situation I shared with her. I appreciated that about her. I understood she had endured trauma, coming from an overly religious background and running away as a teenager, which set the pattern for living on the street.

She eventually met and fell in love with a guitarist at the flea market who had a recording studio in his home. I saw them together on the street, in Pigalle. He had long, curly black hair, with a sullen air about him. She looked smitten, following him like a lost puppy and no longer wearing the fuchsia lipstick. (Maybe he kissed it all off her.) We had grown apart, each in our distinctive musical careers. We spoke momentarily on the street that day, while he waited, with propriety. No longer a nanny, she lived with him, writing songs and recording them in his studio. After that day in Pigalle, I never saw her again.

It was in Paris that I realized how sharing our stories with empathic listeners helps validate and heal our lives. Our shared experiences become less trivial, more valid, and show us—and them—who we are.

22. Panic on the Périphérique

The best kind of horror story is the kind you live to tell.
— Unknown

THERE WERE TIMES IN PARIS WHEN it was an adventure to be utterly lost (*So did that mean that I wasn't lost?*)—or more like untethered by conscious choice. I had reached a certain plateau of success and was contemplating some kind of change.

Returning to Paris from a recent three-week trip to Seattle had left me with an irksome pain in my heart—a sadness about leaving the predictable comforts of home with Tor, my dog, the lake, and the questions from meddling relatives about my life choices. My parents were pleading with me, through long-distance phone calls and letters: "Come home and have children before it's too late!"

In contrast, my brother Norman reminded me, in his melancholy letters, "Stay in Paris, there's nothing for you here."

On the morning of my twenty-ninth birthday, I cut my finger deeply while trying to salvage a stale baguette for breakfast. (Of all times, why wasn't I enjoying breakfast in bed, served by a doting lover?) I could have chosen a flaky croissant instead, but with a plethora of bakeries in one's neighborhood, one quickly learns that eating these delectable, buttery croissants is habit-forming and not conducive to the silhouette of a chanteuse in Paris.

Unable to stop the bleeding, I panicked, running down five flights of stairs, through the street, and around the corner to the quaint, upscale pharmacy. My hand was erratically wrapped in a handy dish towel that was soaking through with blood; surely this would demand everyone's attention!

There was a queue at the pharmacy as I pleaded, *"S'il vous plaît?"* The chic woman pharmacist, looking more like a movie star, gave me that quick, superior gaze and coolly ordered, "Wait your turn." (Ouch! Still, I loved her accent.)

The French are not like Americans when it comes to emergencies. Well, maybe it wasn't a true emergency, but it felt like one.

I couldn't believe her chilly dismissal. Even though I'd lived in Paris for more than two years, this was my first experience with the infamous Parisian hauteur toward foreigners. I just happened to be in her line of fire, the target of her thinly veiled disdain toward the aliens infiltrating her beautiful city.

I wanted to shout, "I WEAR BOAS, DAMN IT, DO YOU KNOW WHAT THAT MEANS?" But it would be too easy to play the victim here. I needed Band-Aids.

Finally, it was my turn and I hadn't passed out. She bandaged up my deep cut, bless her heart (part of a French pharmacist's job description). Bleeding in a pharmacy on my birthday! It was so unglamorous.

. . . .

At the club after my show, the staff and I, including the kitchen help, often hung out having an end-of-the-night drink.

We were a tight group of crazies. Once the pressure of the evening was off, we shared amusing anecdotes and joked about the night's events: the occasional French celebrity, the gradual inebriation of the clientele, friends who'd swung by, and the ludicrous scenarios that transpired. Like when I sat down next to Brian Eno at Stacy's invitation and, not really knowing of his prestige, asked him what he did for a living. He mumbled something that sounded like "I sell oranges."

"Oh, you sell oranges?" I asked.

"I'm an organist!" he replied, carefully enunciating.

"My brother is an organist too!" I chirped (thinking of how much I missed him).

"A captivating career, I'm sure," he responded with a strange, lopsided smile.

He was thin and slight of build, with stringy ash-blond hair. I thought him provocative, in an unwholesome way.

I must have used the wrong opening line to break the ice, as the conversation turned bleak, with no flirting, chemistry, or intrigue going on. (I remembered my brother had warned me: all male organists are gay.) I flitted off to find a more receptive flower. I was an entertainer, a femme fatale, and sullen men made me nervous. I blossomed with guests who appreciated the persona I brought to the table: amusing, unpredictable, and full of French non sequiturs.

One Saturday night, as the evening was winding down and everyone seemed to be going somewhere, for the first time I boldly asked, as I'd noticed others had in the past, "Anyone like to share a taxi to the 20th arrondissement?"

I was house-sitting for a friend for the next few weeks in an unfamiliar, unfashionable neighborhood that no one was going to. The chef—kingpin of the restaurant—laughingly said, "He would love to give you a ride home," pointing with a sly grin toward Sylvain, his less-than-astute, humble sous-chef.

Looking directly into the head chef's eyes, I asked, "Are you sure he knows the way?"

"He knows zee way better zhan you!" Everyone laughed, except me and Sylvain.

Sylvain looked like he might end up behind bars someday and have no idea why. But I assumed that, because the ride home was the chef's suggestion, it would be OK. After all, I was the "star" of the club and everyone wished the best for me.

I realize now that I was oblivious to the dangers that could lurk in foreign men's eyes when they observed me in my role of "provocative

American singer." (*"Foreigner woman, on the loose—she must be loose." "Oui, oui, she must be looking for love, like everyone is in Paris."*)

I drank champagne regularly at the club, as patrons offered invitingly *"une coupe de champagne, jolie Julie?"*—and hey, in Paris, there didn't seem to be anything wrong with it. Except that I was occasionally buzzed, trusting untrustworthy people, and this night was no exception.

Sylvain's lack of English, which hadn't registered in my tipsiness, was about to become a rude awakening, *"Allez-vous, cherie!"* (Let's go, darling!), I said, emptying the last swallow of champagne, which seemed to cinch the deal.

With confidence, I handed Sylvain the address where I anticipated he'd momentarily drop me, as I followed him to his car. (Sylvain owned a car, which was a sign that you had something going for you in France—rich parents or a well-paying job or both.)

I could handle a kitchen assistant while others were around, but now, alone in his car, with him in the driver's seat, I suddenly felt vulnerable. I knew I had that unrealistic American trust that all people in Paris were genteel.

He seemed a capable driver, stopping at red lights, not driving fast. A few minutes into our journey, he turned onto the Périphérique, the French freeway that circles the outer boundaries of Paris. I had experienced this baffling motorway before with friends on Sunday drives to their summer homes. Yes—in those cases, the Périphérique was the thing to do. You could travel long, far, and fast. But this address was in Paris proper! This was something I had no desire to be doing at 1 a.m. on a Saturday night, with this strange dude at the wheel.

Why had I accepted a ride with this unseemly person in the first place?

Just because he worked at the club where I was singing and because his dubious boss (whom, I later found out, was a knucklehead) had recommended him? As the champagne wore off, as it always does, it sunk in what a mistake I'd made. The car sped by signs listing faraway places that I had visited with friends: Rouen, Lourdes, Lyon—were we leaving Paris?

We were far away from all that was familiar to me. I tried to ingratiate myself with him by making small talk in broken French. Men usually seemed to enjoy it. But he was deaf to my words and driving faster. I fell silent. A sick feeling told me something terrible was going to happen. I would have to use every ounce of my luck, cleverness, and pepper spray to get out of this potentially fatal situation.

To break the uncomfortable silence, I spoke calmly, telling him that I would prefer he drove more slowly. Was that too much to ask from a sous-chef giving you a lift? I guess it was, since it incited him to accelerate!

In desperation, I pulled out the over-the-top *"My parents were both killed in a terrible car accident when I was child!"* card, hoping to imply that a traumatic flashback might ensue if he didn't ease off the pedal. Either he didn't understand or he didn't care.

"I was the only survivor of that devastating car crash!" I continued, then pretended to cry, despite how preposterous it sounded. No one who'd been in a horrific accident would have considered getting into a car with a person whose driving skills were unknown. It was too melodramatic to be believed. He had now checked out of the conversation and had no investment in pleasing me.

I imagined he was perversely enjoying my squirming for French words in order to persuade him to slow down. What happened to the nice sous-chef I originally thought he was? I remembered how he had shyly complimented me when I'd come into the kitchen to "see what was cooking."

Now I was under *his* control. A *sitting duck*—an apt description never more fitting to me than at that moment. And to think I arranged this!

With my peripheral vision, I studied his deranged profile. I saw something in that aberrant face . . . was it a glint of evil? Finally, I had the cold realization that he might be abducting me!

From my large "gig bag" I discreetly changed my heels for my walking sandals and miraculously found my small, leather-encased canister of Mace—which I had smuggled into France for such an occasion. I hoped it would do the job. (I should have tried it out before I needed it.) I was preparing to escape as soon as he stopped the car, if not sooner. My heart was beating fast, and I was on high alert, waiting for an opportunity to jump out of the car if he ever slowed down. Where were the gendarmes when a jerk like this was speeding? Nowhere in sight.

Where on earth was he taking me? I was afraid to ask.

I began spiraling into an imagined scenario of him stopping in an isolated field, where dreadful things would happen. I felt overwhelming compassion for the victims of crimes during those last moments of being alive.

I would fight this monster for my life, unless of course he had a knife or a gun? I would blind him with my Mace, leave my large bag behind, and flee with my wallet, keys, and lipstick.

"Oh my God!" I thought.

The tires screeched as he turned abruptly off the Périphérique. This eased part of my tension, yet I didn't recognize anything, because every French neighborhood looked similar. No one was around at this time of the early morning. It must have been after 2 a.m.

Sylvain then pulled over to the side of the road, stood in front of the headlights, and urinated in the pouring rain, just like in a bad French film noir. Relieved for some reason, I remained in his car, now realizing he had no plan to harm me.

As he started to drive again, the scenery became familiar as I squinted through the downpour. There was that typical café, in that obscure, undefined corner where I was staying. I recognized the red fire hydrant across the street.

"That's it!" I screamed. He jammed on the brakes.

Not missing a beat, I jumped out of the car, heavy bag in my arms, and ran to the gate of the building with my keys in hand.

He yelled something strange, *"C'est pas là"* (It's not there), and sped off, like the jackass he was.

Once inside the building, I felt shaken and grateful for this wake-up call. I was a solo woman in a foreign country where I didn't handle the language well enough to use my wits to get out of a sticky situation. I was the only person responsible for my safety at all times. I wasn't a child on vacation in Disneyland, although I acted like one sometimes.

That following week, when I shared my misadventure with my waitress friends at the Hollywood Savoy, they said, *Ah, just another escapade for zee wild American singer!* I felt laughed at and that the experience had not been taken seriously. Or was I not taking my life seriously enough?

Madam Lenora advised me to report it to the owner of the club, but it was a moot point, since nothing really happened. But I had been afraid something would! I knew it in my bones. I would have been a perfect victim: *the sassy singer who thought she had any tiger by the tail.*

When it came right down to it, I was a scared little girl who could only speak enough French to get herself into trouble. When things happened, who could I turn to? I didn't have three helpful brothers or a boyfriend or parents to come to my rescue.

23. Norwegian Twins

*The memory of quality lasts long after
the price has been forgotten.*
— Aldo Gucci

IT WAS THE PARISIAN SUMMER OF '87. I had been back to Seattle for several extended stints, still Paris was increasingly feeling like home. My singing career was established, and I was living life as a madcap musical personality for enthusiastic crowds at *le club du jour*, the Hollywood Savoy.

I had leased an apartment on the Rue Gît-le-Coeur. I was feeling a certain amount of commitment. Unbeknownst to me, downstairs from my apartment on the first floor was the iconic Beat Hotel.

I had no concept of the Beat Generation or what that hotel represented, except that at one time it meant something cool concerning the writers Allen Ginsberg, William S. Burroughs, and Jack Kerouac. One day after I had lived in the neighborhood for a few weeks, I tentatively stepped inside the Beat Hotel out of idle curiosity and quickly walked out. It was a real hotel and a real dump, not emitting one iota of music. I didn't linger—I didn't have to. I had my own apartment upstairs. Decades later I realized Kerouac was one of the awe-inspiring Beat poets who used to hang out there. Finding the iconic hotel, rich with poetic rumblings and syncopated rhythms from days past, had not been a random and lucky happenstance. Again, it was due to the helpful bulletin board at the American Church.

Charmed things happened without my knowing what I was doing. The less aware I was of the potential marvels in my midst, the more likely I was to land in something extraordinary. That's what happens when you leave home and cultivate the intention of pursuing a dream. You step out of your patterns. Take, for instance, the delectable Norwegian twins, Johan and Petter, enchantingly appearing in my life.

Johan lived in Paris at the time. We met at the Savoy, one crazy night when I was in especially good form. An instant kinship ignited between us. I am half Norwegian due to my grandmother on my mother's side. (At that time I was passing for full-blooded Italian, as it was more dramatic, and I kept the Norwegian ancestry on the down-low.) Johan was gay and had left Norway to follow his dream to live in Paris for a year before he got serious about a career. I believed he preferred Paris, far from the disapproving eye of the Scandinavian mindset that one must conform and not be too different from others. The sometimes censorious Norwegian mentality, in general, didn't approve of drawing attention to oneself. Our friendship felt natural in bohemian Paris. He helped put my Norwegian sensibilities in perspective, and it felt acceptable to live with abandon in Paris.

One summery weekend, Johan's identical twin, Petter, came from Oslo for a short visit. It was a treat going around Paris with handsome identical twins who were tall, blond, square-jawed, and masculine. I finally understood how virile a man must feel when two lavishly beautiful women were holding on to his arm. It was Eurotrash glamour with a Nordic twist. The dudes were unusually eye-catching compared to the eclectic, motley fare in Paris.

The weather that weekend was exceptionally warm, so swimming was the only thing to do. The retro Piscine Molitor was my bright idea. The art deco outdoor pool was in decline and, like most monuments, *historique*. Adding to its iconic pizzazz, Johnny Weissmuller, of *Tarzan* fame, had been *filmed* there as a lifeguard.

This pool was my favorite place to swim. But there was something seedy and questionable about the changing rooms; I often wondered what had gone on in them. I hoped they'd been sanitized, though I had my doubts. The pool remained open until the late '80s, until in 1989 it fell into disuse and was boarded up.

Putting our towels down, we planted ourselves by the pool's edge, studying the swimmers and other frolickers as well as sunbathers slathering lotion on themselves and on each other. Petter quietly offered to apply suntan lotion to my back. I felt vaguely shy and wasn't sure I liked a man studying me from that angle. Would I know what to do if he asked me to reciprocate? Why was I timid around this man? As he began massaging the slippery lotion onto my back, I found his touch electrifying. What was going on? I hoped he didn't notice. As a well-brought-up Norwegian man, he made no request for me to reciprocate. I knew Johan was really gay, and until this moment I didn't make the connection that Petter might well be really straight. I thought they might be identically gay!

We were barely in our late twenties, single and still trying to figure out where life was leading us. I imagined we all wanted meaningful lives, and that's what we had in common. I knew very little about them other than that they were polite and magazine-cover adorable, had a family hotel in Oslo, and reminded me affectionately of my Norwegian grandmother.

Foreign artists had long found Paris a sanctuary for self-discovery. And if you remain in Paris long enough (a mysterious stretch of time, deemed by the gods), Paris reveals why you'd been "summoned." Music was the vehicle that chose me to fulfill my visions and hopefully to heal unconscious emotional wounds in myself and the listeners.

Singing gave me something to hang my exuberance upon. It validated my being in Paris, so I could get to the magical messages that music bestows upon the singer to share with others. When I had that crazy, uncontrollable attraction to a song, I believed that the song chose me to sing it. To love, learn, and perform a song is to commit to a deepening process. Songs enter our consciousness to unravel and reveal secrets we didn't know we were keeping. A singer becomes devoted to a song and the mysteries are revealed, leaving us to our destiny.

I had achieved a certain amount of notoriety singing in Parisian clubs and at gala events—like the Bush–Dukakis election-night party at the American Embassy, as well as at several private estates outside Paris and London. It was a high-profile yet financially limited circuit. I wondered what this would lead to if I continued. Was my current success enough to warrant moving to Paris, lock, stock, and lipstick? Or should I return to Seattle and regroup? I wanted more, but I wasn't sure I could create more than this.

Paris and music went together beautifully. That was the fun part of running away from Seattle. I had my demons and felt conflicted, but I hoped those nagging thoughts would keep quiet. I needed momentum before I did too much self-reflection and made a wrong move. I found solace in focusing on being a singer and loved how it consumed me, like a passionate addiction. I wanted to see where this journey would lead me. Paris was a portal . . . leading me where?

. . . .

Petter was celebrating the fact that he had recently recovered from breaking his arm by jumping out of an airplane. (How manly.) This weekend in Paris commemorated the removal after six months of a plaster cast on his right arm, and he was ready to party.

After sitting too long in the sweltering sun, amid the high-spirited chatter at the pool, the boys went to get some cool drinks. As they walked away, I jumped in the pool. The water was invigorating, waking me out of a sun-induced trance. I'd been longing for this immersion into coolness, but the social interactions seemed to take precedence. When the twins returned with the beverages, they happily joined me in the water. The pool was populated by skimpily clad Parisians dressed in their Riviera-style attire.

We played a form of tag—swimming and running slowly with great effort in the pool, grabbing each other's bathing suits, laughing childishly, getting water in our noses. We reverted to simple antics, chasing the multicolored beach ball and playing a version of volleyball with hapless strangers. Someone shouted *"Uff da!"* It had to be one of the Norwegians!

That night, I had a gig at a new club that had just opened. I felt refreshed after the swim and ready for a great night of expression, and the twins said they'd stop by. The club was definitely not the Hollywood Savoy, and the absence of Stacy Macadams's structure gave me a chance to relax and interact with the audience on my own terms, as if I were entertaining in my home.

"Any requests?" I purred.

Someone yelled, "Copacabana!" That was one of my standards in Paris. I had an interesting set list that night that included "Cabaret," "New York, New York," and "You Made Me Love You."

The twins arrived rested and in a jovial mood. As the night progressed, Petter overcame his reserve toward me. Was it the alcohol? Or had he finally realized I was the spicy dish of pasta he'd been hankering for? No longer just a casual, fun, brotherly friend, he let his gaze linger as we bantered. I wasn't expecting it. I had cultivated tactics to dissuade such attentions in Paris, but there's a weak link in every chain.

A plethora of men had pursued me in Paris. They sensed I was on display for them to peruse my glamor, my love of life, and my romantic songs—who could resist? That evening, after my show and a few drinks, we were walking to our respective abodes when Petter offered to see me home.

What a well-bred gentleman, I thought, *the kind I've always wanted.*

I had a daybed that was more than comfortable for him to stay on, if that was on the agenda.

Was it because he was Norwegian, and his accent reminded me of my kindly grandmother, whom I adored and trusted? Or because I knew his brother Johan so well that I transferred that familiarity onto his cute Viking brother? I didn't understand my throwing caution out the window and trusting him utterly.

We talked most of the night. He told me about his devotion to the mountain topography of Norway, how much he loved helping others in need, and that he was soon to become a medical emergency pilot. He was natural, calm, and capable of knowing what to do in any situation. He had a way about him that I liked more than a little. He was the kind of man I wanted but never seemed to come into contact with. Was this becoming a crisis he must manage in the darkness of my rooftop apartment atop the Beat Hotel?

He was ready for a fling, and I secretly wanted more. We decided to leave it as just friends.

In the morning, as he slept, I made coffee, saying softly under my breath, *"Jei elska deg,"* the only thing I knew how to say in Norwegian. It was a declaration of love for him to either pretend he didn't hear, or possibly to take notice of. Like when my grandmother used to whisper it to me, her closest grandchild, as I drifted off to sleep. It felt safe to express this sentiment, as I knew I'd never see him again.

He embraced me and told me how much he'd enjoyed getting to know me, dressed quickly, and left. A little voice in my head told me I was too busy to feel bad, although I had wanted more than *"hade bra"* (a familiar Norwegian phrase for "go well").

It felt more like he had just checked out of the Beat Hotel.

Over the years, I've never forgotten him. I stored this memory in a new category best expressed by the great poet Bob Marley: "The truth is everyone is going to hurt you. You just got to find the ones worth suffering for."

24. Rue Gît-le-Coeur

*Our memories are scattered all over the world,
we just have to find them.*
— Unknown

NO MATTER WHAT SEASON IN PARIS, at certain times an invisible elixir in the air made you feel that you had to be in love. I'd been in Paris almost three years, occasionally leaving it for work in London and various gala events. Trips to the States to see family and check in with Tor were wearing thin. He wasn't as trusting of this long-distance relationship or of my success as he once had been. Yet I still considered Seattle my real home, and our dog, Sophie, kept our relationship intact.

My current apartment, on the Rue Gît-le-Coeur, was more expensive than my previous situations, but everything I needed was in the neighborhood. My talents were in demand, especially at the Hollywood Savoy. It became my touchstone each time I returned to Paris. Now, when I'd occasionally visit Seattle, people would hear I was "making it big" there and wonder if I might stay there forever.

When I'd originally headed to Paris, numerous friends in Seattle offered pleasant introductions to people they knew who currently lived in Paris. I had bonded willingly with many of these eccentric foreigners and world travelers.

Until recently, a man known as Captain James had been the last such contact I had checked off my list. He had been recommended by

Jerry Lewis (not the comedian), a former coworker of mine at the Pike Place Cinema in Seattle, one of my happier part-time jobs. Jerry was the projectionist; I sold tickets and made popcorn. He suggested that I might rendezvous with his former landlord, Captain James. Before I came to Paris, Jerry had rented the cheapest of "cabins" from Captain James aboard the *Klaidonis*, a renovated coal barge, which Parisians called a *péniche*. I liked the intrigue and drama of meeting someone who lived on a *péniche* in the Seine. I preferred walking alongside the river rather than the sidewalks when I had the option. A feeling of the real Paris embraced me in those wanderings.

Since the Rue Gît-le-Coeur was parallel to the Seine, I often walked the quay and would stop to say hello to Captain James. One afternoon, I'd left numerous telephone messages for friends and acquaintances, hoping I might entice someone to meet me that evening at the gala party and vernissage at Le Palace for the American painter Daniel Cueva. I hated going to glamorous events alone, but no one had responded yet.

Instead of going solo, I reluctantly thought I'd stay home and work on my music. Now that would be a novel experience in those days. I was living in the fast lane, in a cultural hotbed of art, fashion, music, film, theater, and parties! Performing was where I practiced my art. It was de rigueur to have plans every night and be part of the "scene." And Le Palace was the premier nightclub in Paris. Daniel Cueva, quick to exaggerate, exclaimed, "This will be a spectacular event you don't want to miss!"

Every night of my life at the Hollywood Savoy was a "spectacular event"; I could live without another party, couldn't I?

I'd met Daniel Cueva at the Paris Art School, where he held a desirable teaching residency. Originally from San Diego, California, he became a good friend. He was gay, of course! I found gay men exciting, congenial, and less distracting than straight men. During my brother Norman's sporadic invitations into the gay world, I was captivated by his friends, who taught me the appeal of sardonic humor, joie de vivre, and the complete absence of romantic tension (they didn't want to sleep with me).

Daniel Cueva, the American Picasso, created exquisite painted fabric for haute couture designers. The evening promised to be remarkable, with impressive names in attendance. There would also be an array of up-and-coming stylish artists in the Paris art scene, plus paparazzi! That in itself meant "fabulous"!

It was a gorgeous afternoon, drenched in languid late-day sunlight. It seemed a pleasant idea to have a short visit with Captain James, a slightly built, youthful-looking retired professor from Latvia. I'd had a few visits with him but never understood what he was doing in Paris other than living on his barge. Whenever I dropped by, he welcomed me with a glass of tepid white wine or an espresso. My outgoing American demeanor clashed with his somewhat confused masculine sensibility. We sat in the simple salon of his craft. I noticed, when he turned away, that he'd circled an advertisement for "Asian Girls" in his opened magazine on the table where he had precisely placed my wine.

I had no idea how he got moorage on the Seine; real estate conversations didn't come up in Paris like they did in the States. And I didn't really care. I was into art and music and getting gigs.

We'd talk about traveling and cruise ships and writers and worries. He said people invent worries if they have none. I wondered if that comment was meant for me. Sure, I worried plenty (like, Was I frittering my free time away running around Paris visiting eccentric oddballs like him?). Often, Captain James shared meaningless information with me—for example, that there was a new *péniche* moored nearby as of recently, and he thought they were from Holland! *Should I care for some reason?* I wondered.

After the quick drink and bland conversation, it was time to move on. James always instigated the end of our visits. It seemed he couldn't sit still for long, which was a welcome relief.

As I continued my lonesome stroll along the Seine, I glimpsed a stunning black-and-gray *péniche* like a pirate ship, its grand sails gently swaying in the wind: the *Leontyne*, it was called. I noticed a bulky, sandy-haired man about to duck into the steering cabin, so I called out, recalling the inane conversation with Captain James, "Hey, are you from Holland?"

He turned quickly, smiling, and said, "No, I'm from England. Where are you from?"

"Seattle!"

With a friendly wave, he called out, "Well, come aboard. Have a drink!"

I hesitated for a second and jumped on. I was getting good at jumping on and off boats. I had recently performed on a cruise ship for three weeks, not to mention the visits on the *Klaidonis* down the river. Was life beginning to take me in a nautical direction?

The *Leontyne* had been converted into a movie studio! Film canisters, cameras, silver umbrella reflectors. The setup was elegant and professional, including a casting couch!

Even though considerably older than I, with a large paunch, Richard Goodwin asked me if I wanted to go out for dinner. I had learned that in Paris it's best to know someone before dining with them. A man and woman sharing food together in Paris was an intimate exchange, the next step being an eventual walk to the bedroom. But he wasn't French and he didn't seem like a letch. As we chatted, he informed me that he was making a film about traveling by barge through Europe. That particular evening, he had been on his way to visit the singer who was supposed to be in his current segment of the film but was hospitalized due to just having had a stroke.

"Are you kidding?" I almost choked on the heavenly chilled wine I was sipping!

Had he been tipped off that I, Julie Cascioppo, American chanteuse, semi-famous, relatively new to the Paris music scene, always looking for singing engagements, was passing by just in the nick of time to save his film? Could this really be happening? Kismet!

"I'm a singer!" I chimed.

He studied me. "No, really?" (This was all too perfect and cosmically aligned!)

We chatted, sipping wine and nibbling cheese, lounging on the

Adirondack chairs on the *Leontyne*'s deck. He ripped open a bag of lettuce to munch as he divulged details about his film in progress. The crew had finished for the day. I hung on to every word as my imagination ran wild. *This could be my big break!* I could skip singing altogether and become a cult movie star in Europe. I thought he might be gay, but it's hard to tell with Englishmen. They're sexy, in a prissy way.

As the conversation unfolded, he shared that he'd grown up in India but was educated in New York City. We seemed to be communicating with great ease and excitement.

"Do you think you could sing a French song some afternoon this week, while we film you?"

I eagerly replied, "I'd love to!"

As a PBS Special his plan was to make it seem like he simply happened to discover a woman unselfconsciously singing on the quay.

Now that we were acquainted, I audaciously offered, "I'm going to a party at Le Palace tonight. It's a vernissage for my artist friend Daniel Cueva. Perhaps you'd like to go?" Now that he no longer had to check on the other singer, he was free, and he had me!

His acceptance surprised me, since so many others hadn't responded. (*You'll hear a hundred nos and then one yes.* —Chinese proverb)

After the wine, I said I'd run home and put on something artsy, and then come back and fetch him.

"Won't that be a big bore to come back? I'll come fetch you."

I scribbled down my address, 13 rue Gît-le-Coeur. He looked at me and ordered with the confidence of a Svengali, "Wear your hair up."

That was a first. No man ever told me how to wear my hair, unless he was my hairdresser.

I ran home to transform—my place was near—and I was suddenly insufferably happy! Now I could go to the party with a date, and I'd wear one of Daniel's creations.

In addition to painting on canvas, Daniel specialized in fabric painting. He was involved with haute couture designers Patrick Kelly, Calvin Klein, and many others beyond my scope. During our friendship,

Daniel gave me two of his gowns, whispering, "Don't tell a soul I gave these to you! I'm not supposed to give them away!"

While dressing for the party, I realized I would have hated missing this event. Tonight I would wear one of Daniel's gowns and his secret would be safe with me.

Nothing else mattered to me at that moment. I had a date, I was in a couture dress, and on Richard's suggestion, I wore my hair up.

We taxied to Le Palace, the hottest dance club in Paris, catering to celebrities like Grace Jones and Rudolf Nureyev, both of whom I actually saw there that evening. It was "the" spot, with doormen whose sole purpose was to screen out undesirables who weren't chic enough—which didn't include me, as I had a personal invitation!

The champagne flowed. It was more than an event, it was a happening. We walked into a kaleidoscope of beautiful people, who sized us up with big eyes. We were a striking couple; I felt like an actress, with an air of power and authority, escorted by her distinguished movie director.

By chance, we ran into my friend Rochelle and her dangerously attractive Italian lover, Cosimo. They appeared to have had a serious conversation before the event, rehashing their usual point of contention with each other. He was an aspiring actor and Rochelle wanted him to father her children. He feared he couldn't do both. I could relate.

I introduced my director friend to them, which led to much speculation, I hoped. I was realizing that who people thought you were sleeping with in Paris was much more important than who you actually slept with.

We ran into Daniel Cueva, his eyes bulging out of his head with excitement and overstimulation. He made a fuss about my showing up in a beautiful gown that he'd painted, kissing me on both cheeks. Surrounded by his entourage, he was definitely in his element, and his show was an overwhelming success.

My life was unfolding like the fairy tale I'd secretly fantasized it could be, and the champagne helped! I felt enfolded in divine light, surrounded by extraordinarily dressed movers and shakers.

I really liked my new director/producer friend. I thought to myself, *I must find out more about him.* He was too old for me, but that didn't matter. He had the *je ne sais quoi* I required in a man . . . magnetism, creativity, and class.

At the end of the evening he kissed my hand goodnight and repeated his request that I sing in his film, the PBS Special on barge travel through Europe. I was thrilled, as if I'd been given the starring role in *Romeo and Juliet*.

The next day, he moved fast staging my sequence at a small cabaret table on the quay. Wearing my skintight polka-dot toreador pants, I dramatically sang a version of "La Vie en Rose." I didn't particularly love how the recording of the song went. I was outdoors on the Seine without a sound system. A French accordionist accompanied me. It seemed Richard wanted me to appear to be a bohemian, singing canal wench, that he met spontaneously along the Seine—which I wasn't. I was a dynamic singer who wanted to be discovered, utilized, and adored.

Alas, I was simply part of a contrived landscape. He was designing a natural-seeming ambience, like "This is what happens every day on the banks of the Seine when you travel by barge through Paris, and it's all so magical."

I was excited and intensely interested by my growing friendship with Mr. Goodwin. I hoped my life could mysteriously change in an instant, from simply singing in French jazz clubs and bars to being in films through this creative English director.

One day, shortly after my film debut, I went to the river to say hello.

The *Leontyne* and crew were gone!

I felt a jab in my heart. I presumed they moved somewhere farther down the Seine, or possibly had left Paris completely.

The reality was I had been an incidental character who showed up on cue. He got the musical shot he was looking for and then simply disappeared, never to know of my outlandish fantasy.

I returned to my apartment puzzled and sad, as I readied myself for my regular singing engagement. Slowly I applied my evening makeup, more boldly than usual—darker, thicker eyeliner; bigger, redder lips. I figured we might possibly meet again somehow, somewhere. He knew where I was singing.

· · · · · · · · · · · · · · · · ·

Daniel Cueva died of AIDS in 1987 when he was thirty-six years old. I was proud of him and his career. He had courage. He was one of my very first friends to perish from AIDS.

25. Fontainebleau Fantasy

Traveling is exploring other people's realities.
— Unknown

A T ONE OF THE MANY VERNISSAGES held in the Paris art world, Daniel Cueva introduced me to the petite, bubbly Christian. He was *gentil*, cherubically handsome, with a countenance that seemed to hearken back to another era. He definitely belonged in the world of theater, and that was his life.

Soon after Daniel's typically overblown introduction, Christian and I became friends. Daniel gushed to others that I was his "famous singer friend." And why not? I looked famous. He introduced me lavishly as "the fabulous singer from the States—who has come to Paris to sing!"

I found that, in Paris in the '80s, you simply met people, things clicked, and voilà, you were good friends. It was a benefit of living in that era. There was so much potential and so little reason to be afraid of it. My social life was spontaneous and unpredictable and that seemed to be the best way to navigate life there.

One day, Christian invited me over for coffee. He lived in a large apartment in the Palais-Royal, across the street from the Louvre. I had heard that the Palais-Royal was a former royal palace that was later turned into an arcade where the wealthy and genteel could go for *très cher* shopping. Little did I know it also housed theaters, restaurants, gardens, galleries, bookstores, and an opera house. No one could possibly live there, it seemed, but Christian and a few others did. It was a historic landmark, and the apartments were inherited by the relatives of the original families from hundreds of years ago.

Christian worked in the film and theater industry procuring extraordinary props, restoring them, and keeping them in working order. His apartment was crammed full of remarkable curios, antiques both dusty and brilliant, and objets d'art! There were grand oil paintings, both copies and originals, from generations of collecting and curating. All the objects presented diverse aspects of French culture, conveying story and setting. It was an esoteric mish-mash of French history. Christian had inherited the large flat from his family. Property is handed down in the family line because the family name holds high esteem in European culture when it's attached to property.

Our conversation was breezy and light, sprinkled with comfort and humor. That personal, safe connection that I felt with gay men propelled this lovely visit. Having traveled for his career, he was sensitive that I was alone, far from my home of origin. I sensed he loved people who made him laugh, and we had a mutual appreciation for each other's humor. It helped that his English was excellent.

He offered me a cup of coffee, and I imagined he'd make a superb one, as that was the original premise of this invitation. I watched in awe sitting in his quaint kitchen as he lit a match to the gas stove and warmed up what was left in his old-fashioned coffeepot. For some reason, I appreciated that he let me see that. He wasn't particularly wealthy, and I understood hating to throw out good coffee when it just needed a little warming up.

We hadn't built much of a friendship yet, but that didn't seem to matter. This was the beginning. I believed my background in theater and being a performer helped create a bond more readily. (Theater people tend to like each other.) I was impressed that Christian had invited me into his home and showed me that kindness. Europeans by nature are somewhat wary of strangers, but older French people graciously recounted how well loved Americans were, due to our having saved them during World War II. More than once, I was told tearfully how relieved they were to see the

Americans landing on the beach in Normandy. The United States had been their savior. I was touched deeply and felt pride in being American.

After coffee, Christian wanted to show me a special place where he worked in Fontainebleau, a wooded forest outside Paris. We took the metro from a station that was practically outside his front door, then a train, and in about forty minutes we arrived at what seemed like an extensive farm in the woods. He spoke to a worker in boots and work clothes, making some kind of arrangement. It would be just us, and I had no idea what I was in for . . . some kind of surprise. I somehow trusted him completely but was astounded that he was going to so much trouble for me.

The forest of Fontainebleau was breathtaking. It had miles of winding paths and trails for carriages and horseback riding. Christian explained the stables were utilized for international film locations. I noticed intent workers scuttling about in preparation for, I imagined, future productions. Christian introduced me to the staff and let them know we'd be going for a ride, as the available coachman climbed obediently into the driver's seat. Christian helped me into the carriage and I simply followed directions, hoping for the best.

It was a lovely, brisk day, and in the open carriage we were surrounded by the great outdoors. Trees canopied the trails, making me feel like I was stepping into the fairytale world from the pages of Narnia. I surrendered to the zeal bubbling up, awakening my inner child.

We dashed along paths with low-hanging mossy green foliage. Occasionally I ducked, which made Christian laugh.

"Don't worry, *chérie*, the driver knows *le chemin très bien* (the path well). It has been used in many films."

I replied, "I hope you're not taking me on a joyride that I'll pay for with a head injury!" Soon we were laughing, noticing hedgehogs and other forest creatures as I sang "Just hear those sleigh bells jingling, ting ting tingling too..."

It was like a movie, only better. I had to pinch myself, asking, *Am I really doing this?* I felt in my whole being that this day would become an indelible memory—not just the ride, but Christian's kindness, and how being in the present moment came so naturally with him.

He taught me something important about myself: I could be sought after as company. Someone could treasure me, whether I was "entertaining" or just being me; and on some level, this helped assuage my recurring self-doubts. Yes, I struggled with the uncertainty of being an "artist," but when the gifts appeared, they were beguiling, and made me feel that I was doing *something* right! Gifts like the breathtaking outing through the forests of Fontainebleau.

Things like this could not have happened had I remained safe at home in Seattle. As the saying goes, "A boat must leave port before it finds treasures on other shores."

26. New York Debut

*More tears are shed over answered
prayers than unanswered ones.*
— Truman Capote, quoting Saint Teresa of Avila

SUDDENLY THE HOLLYWOOD SAVOY was purchased by someone new and was closing for a month. I didn't have another steady gig at the moment, and the prospects in Paris weren't that promising. I flew home to Seattle, with a plan to eventually return to Paris.

In Seattle, I picked up where I'd left off, at my quasi "ongoing" engagement at the Pink Door. Summer in Seattle was the best time with tourists stopping by on their way to Alaska, and I was a perfect fit for this lovable, iconic Italian restaurant/cabaret in the Pike Place Market. They always made room for me.

I added some new characters that had bubbled up overseas: Fifi la Rue, the French tour guide, who had a superior attitude toward Americans and made fun of their barbaric ways; Katinka from Helsinka, the wacky cruise-ship director, who came up with zany games for passengers to amuse themselves with; and Sam Turner, the racetrack grifter and gigolo who met the best kind of ladies cruising through the Baltic on his dinghy. These characters sailed smoothly into the Julie Cascioppo Experience, live at the Pink Door.

I was fortunate to have the accomplished Linda Dowdell as my accompanist. At that time, she was the rehearsal pianist for the soon-to-be-famous Mark Morris Dance Group. We had worked together throughout the '80s when I was flying between Paris and Seattle often enough to lose count of my trips. I was grateful to Linda for introducing me to the world of dance and genius. Knowing the Mark Morris Group was an intimate brush with legitimate showbiz and a turning point for me.

After their arduous daily rehearsals, Mark and the dancers would come to see my show at the Pink Door. They'd let off steam with cocktails and belly laughs watching and participating in my quirky act of unlikely characters. (Their unbridled enthusiasm brought out the unconventional screwball in me!) They marveled at what "personas" I might be serving up that night, and what throwback songs from the '60s and '70s I'd render to enhance the theme of my wacky vignettes. I loved having peers in the audience, as they paid nonjudgmental, focused attention and laughed heartily at my quips. This inspired us both.

During my Seattle show, when I shouted out, "Grab a partner, male, female, or neutered!" or "Come on, everybody, let's form a human chain!"—*they actually did!* Their energetic sense of the absurd turned the Pink Door into a wild, Felliniesque party, exactly what Jackie, the sometimes-shy proprietor, hoped for. Jackie secretly revealed to me that I was her alter ego and she was glad to have me back.

Mark was in the throes of moving his company to New York, which included grooming Linda as an all-encompassing music director to go with him and his dancers. He swept her right out from under me at the Pink Door! She was meant for bigger things; but then, so was I.

My lesson in losing Linda was that good accompanists are rare. It's a highly specialized talent to keep up with a singer's deliveries and impromptu departures from the material.

Mark, always a class act, compensated me with an invitation to *open* for his upcoming show, *Mythologies*, at the Manhattan Ballroom in New York City. Linda and I would be reunited onstage in New York in early spring.

His offer was a turning point in my career. I was scared beyond belief and immediately accepted it. It was the only thing to do! I was on a roll. I was wanted in Paris, Seattle, and now New York!

Mark and his company were on a trajectory to stardom in the dance world. New York loved him. His concept was for me to perform my cabaret act as the preshow entertainment, to warm up the audience and get them into a receptive mood for *Mythologies*, and then continue to entertain during the two intermissions. He definitely wanted cabaret. Linda cryptically assured me "If Mark had wanted Patti LuPone, he would have hired her. But he chose you." That sounded like a compliment to me.

"What would you like me to do?" I asked Mark, anticipating that he would want me to work up something new and even better than what I'd been improvising at the Pink Door for years.

"Just do your usual fabulous show, Julie!" (*Easier said than done in New York,* I thought.) I wondered if my sense of humor would register with a New York audience. I could have shouted, "I'm not ready for New York yet!" But I was not about to reveal any insecurities, and I needed to accept the fact that he knew what he'd be getting.

Knowing myself, I would never feel what I considered "ready." But by this time in my life, my thirties, I knew that when an opportunity comes your way, *you better reach out and grab it!*

In Seattle, I was confident in small, noisy cabarets and bars, filled with friends, fans, relatives, and some out-of-towners. I preferred an audience who appreciated my off-the-cuff improvisations. Working out every character's psychological perplexities was giving me and my audience psychotherapy, and we didn't even know it.

Mark's generous invitation was critical because it would be my New York debut in a prestigious theater. Without negotiation, they provided my flight, a private hotel room near the venue, and a per diem for all five nights of performing. Plus, they paid union scale for a Broadway performer! Even though Linda was now living in New York, she was psyched to be my accompanist.

Behind my bravado was that constant pull of uncertainty mixed with impostor syndrome. But I would do it anyway. That's how I'd cure that critical voice: just do the gig. But I was lost about how to prepare myself for this unprecedented exposure of my act. I suspected that a New York audience would expect nothing less than a virtuoso. I scared myself through spinning tales, in my head, of the magnitude of New York and the people in it.

There was no one quite like me: a dedicated singer, a quirky personality, and a work in progress, and Mark got that. I wanted to be dynamic and self-assured as an artist and own what I was doing, because I loved sharing it. Doggone it, where was my audacity when I needed it? Where was my Svengali? I wanted someone to tell me what to do, so I could argue with them and then insist on doing what I wanted.

I'd never utilized outside help before, but I needed someone now. I asked a few Seattle theater luminaries, but it seemed as though everyone I knew was in the same boat and couldn't think of anyone who could help me. Since I had no one to turn to for the guidance and encouragement I needed so badly, I gave it to myself.

I would do this show come hell or high water and be the idiosyncratic cabaret act I was famous for in Seattle. I'd blow those mysterious New York sophisticates right out of the Manhattan Ballroom! If Paris found me entertaining, well, then, so would New York.

In Seattle, I had six weeks to prepare my act. I practiced on my own, studying lyrics and working on my past material. I woodshedded with a variety of pickup pianists who had no understanding of the importance of my impending New York engagement.

For the first time, I was in this unique position of being the opening act for someone—someone the audience was *dying* to see! So far this hadn't occurred in my performance scenarios. I had good reason to be shaking in my stilettos, still pretending to be "cool." I reminded myself, Mark would not have made me part of this world premiere in New York if he had doubts. I loved the entire company. Since they didn't doubt me, I could just pretend I was doing it *for them*, which I was! (During my performances, they were able to change costumes and drink a glass of water.)

Mark wanted what he saw me do in Seattle: be a strolling cabaret singer, wearing a Jiffy Pop–like silver turban, or an oversized wig, or some other preposterous headpiece. I was to take the audience by surprise and gleefully engage them with whatever popped into my head. All this would transpire while I was gliding through the crowd with the freedom provided by a cordless microphone.

· · · · · · · · · · · · · · · · ·

On opening night, I sensed that the audience members, ravenously flocking to see Mark Morris, weren't exactly sure what to make of me. But, knowing Mark had to have had something to do with this, they showed a certain receptivity. They stood with their drinks or sat at small cabaret tables chatting noisily. My first set featured me in a signature scarlet dress with a white pageboy wig and a red French feathered hat. I took a leisurely spotlit musical stroll through the audience to warm up the crowd, singing, joking, and asking people, "Where are you from tonight?" This kind of performance wasn't for the faint of heart. I was definitely earning my money.

Just before I went on, the frantic stage manager informed me that the fire department would be making a random inspection in the theater. I must tell the audience not to smoke—otherwise, they would immediately close down the venue. (Smoking in public was still tolerated then.) While strolling through the endless labyrinth of distorted and unfamiliar faces, I puzzled over how to enlighten the hyped-up audience with élan and grace. After singing "It's All Right with Me," and adding, "Except smoking, that's NOT ALL RIGHT!" I noticed an animated, overweight bald man with big glasses, blatantly smoking while waving his hand in the air. I imagined he'd be fun to interact with. As I approached him, I purred into the microphone, "Please don't smoke, you might burn the place down, then what will we do?"

He turned awkwardly toward me, sneering, and said, "Don't be a policeman! We'll smoke if we want to."

His rude comment stunned me and I momentarily lost my hard-won sense of bravado. I was trying my best to be charming, amusing, and helpful. I thought, *What a jerk.* I was tempted to slap his face, like they did in some of my favorite films. Instead, I regained my star stature and wandered into oblivion, wishing I were in Paris, where everyone smoked and there were no rules for me to enforce. That would be the last time I mentioned smoking. Let the theater burn down tonight. I was always in the mood to meet eligible firemen!

Then, like a guardian angel, along came that long, tall, cool drink of water, Tommy Tune, a good friend of Mark's. He was in great demand—as a singer, dancer, choreographer, and director. At that time, he had a hit show on Broadway and had won numerous Tonys.

He reached out to hug me, saying with genuine Texan charm, "You are amazingly entertaining and funny!"

If he only knew how vulnerable I felt at that moment, and how grateful I was for the gift of his generous compliment. I love show people. They are change makers in painful situations.

At that moment, thankfully, the master of ceremonies announced Mythologies was about to begin. I would have a half-hour break to recalibrate and come out as someone new.

For my second act, I had changed into a comical character, wearing an extraordinarily long black wig and Jiffy Pop silver turban. The curtain opened dramatically, with a spotlight on me as I sat on the lip of the stage, casually, with one leg underneath me, the other leg dangling over the edge, showing only one shiny yellow high heel. I'm not sure what inspired that unnatural position—probably an off-the-cuff suggestion from one of the helpful stagehands.

I was also wearing a mountain of crinolines, a gimmicky idea borrowed from Madonna. I hoped I looked like I was sitting on a cloud, dreaming of being swept away.

The only problem, though, is that in high heels, without a dance partner, it's tremendously difficult to stand up from a sitting position on the floor holding a cordless microphone!

As I finished the Woody Woodpecker theme song, I attempted to stand up, and one of my spiked canary heels caught in the hem of my crinoline. (Where was that helpful stagehand when I needed him?) The epitome of a wrong moment to try out "new blocking and stage business."

My mind was racing: "Should I use this as my shtick?" My gorgeous heels were holding me hostage, and now I despised them. Then there was the punishing realization that, if I were a real comedian and owning the moment, I could have done all sorts of physical stuff: rolled over, kicked my feet in the air, taken my shoes off . . .

Miraculously, my heel dislodged from the crinoline. Placing the microphone gently on the floor, I proceeded to roll over onto my hands and knees like a playful dog, lifted myself up, and picked up the mic. Oblivious, Linda had kept the show moving, replaying the intro to "Walkin' after Midnight" several times, with the greatest of gusto, until I finally launched into the song as if nothing had happened. Live and learn: if you don't learn, you won't live too long in show business.

. . . .

The Mark Morris Dance Group was a gigantic success with rave reviews. The *Village Voice* gave me a compassionate review: "There are several bars, and cabaret singer Julie Cascioppo entertains the audience before the show and during the intermissions. Adopting a number of warmhearted personas, with improbable outfits to match (one involves an immense turban and a mushroom of a silk skirt), she sings sultry songs and delivers patter so subtly tacky that it reeks of intelligent planning. (She gets all smarmy with a Frenchman; she gushes over the wonderful dancers; she tells how she met Morris in their native Seattle: 'He was the only one would get up and make a human chain with me . . .')."

The dance critic from the *New York Times* unceremoniously stated, "Julie Cascioppo seems not to have decided just how campy she wants her cabaret act to get, but she was skillfully accompanied by Linda Dowdell."

Ouch! Quietly taking the review personally, I never brought it up. Years later, rereading the brief comment, I realized that it was accurate: during that period of my career, I was torn between performing as a "campy, brassy broad" and as a serious, emotive cabaret singer. The scrutiny of a New York stage rattled me. It was easier to go for the laughs and safer for me to have goofy personas and humor to hide behind.

Performing in New York had been one of my goals and I had seized the opportunity. But Paris had fully embraced me and was kinder, so I headed back. My fans and friends were asking for me; I had offers. My philosophy has become "Go where they want you." I returned to the Hollywood Savoy, as well as other venues like Régine's, Duc des Lombards, Le Bilboquet, and Aux Trois Mailletz, where life continued to unfold.

27. Defrosting the Cold War, on the Dance Floor

Dream what you have to dream.
They have been dreamed for you. — Unknown

BACK IN PARIS, I HAD ALMOST FORGOTTEN about opening for the Mark Morris Dance Group in New York two years earlier. Now, suddenly someone would bring that scenario back into focus. I had a surprise visit from my former accompanist, Linda Dowdell—currently Mark Morris's music director. Since our Pink Door days, she had blossomed into a sophisticated world-class musician. The Mark Morris Dance Group had now become (for the three years in Belgium) the Monnaie Dance Group/Mark Morris. I had been summoned to Brussels to perform for the cast party of the final show of the season "for old times' sake."

Linda told me, "There promises to be a fun closing-night party where we can perform excerpts from our iconic cabaret act in Seattle for the dancers! We can do some of our hits from the Pink Door, like 'Born to Be Wild,' 'From Russia with Love,' and 'I Told Ya I Love Ya, Now Get Out'!" She added, "And they'll pass the hat," knowing this group would be more than generous.

I was beginning to appreciate being in demand, although I still enjoyed doing things for fun. This was a chance to rub shoulders with Mark and see all the dancers again. We'd become friends through our performances over the years. It was the closing night of the season.

We rendezvoused at the Gare du Nord and took the high-speed train to Brussels. I recall relaxing on the train, thinking, *I guess my life is an exciting adventure.* But living the dream is a lot of work! I was schlepping suitcases filled with regalia, accessories, and makeup, and I had no idea where I'd be staying. With someone fabulous, I hoped.

I'd heard Mikhail Baryshnikov might show up for the party. I packed the music for "Moscow Nights" as well as "From Russia with Love." I asked myself, *Why should Baryshnikov make me nervous? If he's there, I'll play it cool; and if he's not, it'll be just like any other gig I've ever done, full of surprises.*

There certainly was talk he'd be showing up at some point. As Linda shared with me earlier over a quick espresso, "He's got a lot of cute goin' on!"

She'd been playing for him for the last couple of months. During an interim work junket to Florida, they were photographed in the Everglades by Annie Leibovitz, Linda in a one-piece bathing suit, sitting at a grand piano, and Misha (as he was called by friends) on top, striking a pose. It's become an iconic photograph.

. . . .

The dancers had transformed the spacious room in the back of the Théâtre Royal de la Monnaie into the after-party. The lights were low and vitality was high, the party heading into full swing. Needing no introduction, Linda and I opened with "Born to Be Wild," continuing with "Gypsies, Tramps and Thieves," "Baby Don't Go," and Anita O'Day's "I Told Ya I Love Ya, Now Get Out."

There is nothing quite as exhilarating as a party with dancers, especially when they don't have to save themselves for the next performance. They brought out all the good stuff! Hot, soulful Motown music from their New York collections, the kind no one can resist. There were mind-altering cocktails, whipped up by Guillermo, star bartender, one of Mark's favored male leads; flattering lighting; and guacamole! Pot-enhanced cigarettes smoldered in a communal ashtray, all this combined with their natural wild abandon, made it one of the most memorable parties of my life.

In the shadows, I heard Mark's animated laughter, surrounded by friends; the Season was over, a challenging but successful run! I could feel my show was bringing back happy memories from the nights at the Pink Door. The dancing was winding down—laughing, crying, and carrying on after their lengthy sojourn in Brussels.

Since Baryshnikov might be there, I was raring to launch into my passionate rendition of "Dark Eyes." Back in Seattle I'd charmed the visiting Russian dignitaries at office parties and "Moscow Nights" also came in handy more than once.

I strategically opened the second set with "From Russia with Love." I secretly hoped Baryshnikov would be there to hear my Russian rendition.

For my finale, in my phonetic Russian, I slowly began to sing, *"Nish lish nee sadooo dasha shor roggeee"* (from "Moscow Nights").

I felt the vibe in the room shift. I pretended I didn't notice. But I knew he was there—and I hoped this song would mean something to him. As I finished the number, the room erupted into applause. "Moscow Nights" was just the spice the group needed to remind them how much they appreciated Misha. He walked up to me and looked into my eyes and charmingly said, "You made my night!"

I sensed he meant it. *He was so sexy.* I wanted to sing all night for him.

How many singers can say they made Baryshnikov's night? I felt I'd been crowned 'Queen B.'

His words found an untouched place in my heart. His presence was magnetic and he was maddeningly cute! I couldn't help but imagine there just might be a chance he found me attractive. I knew he and Jessica Lange had called it quits. I allowed myself to melt into a delirium. The recorded music started again and the dancers parked their drinks on the nearest flat surface (never the floor). The camaraderie and love of the dancers for each other, for Misha, and even for me was infectious.

Dancers were my kind of people.

Was I actually part of this?

The DJ took us deeper into the ecstasy of music with Prince's seductive song "Kiss." "You don't have to be beautiful to turn me on . . ."

As the lyrics grooved, "I just need your body, baby, from dusk till dawn," suddenly Misha danced slowly toward me.

He moved rhythmically, subtly—didn't even have to dance and he was dancing! He'd been part of the ensemble all season. They were family. I was the outsider, not quite sanctioned to enter this sacred circle. My body conquered my uncertainty and I began a subtle Cuban motion, left over from my days as a Fred Astaire dance instructor. Dancers communicate physically, and Misha was speaking to me.

Should I consider this an invitation? Yes!

I was taller, but he made up for it in his command of the moment. He had an indescribable attraction that was affecting me.

"You don't need experience, to turn me out; just leave it all up to me I'll show you what it's all about . . ." sang Prince.

I thought, *Yeah, now I know what Prince was singing about*. If you have animal magnetism and are one of the best dancers in the world, anything can happen, and usually does.

As he faced me, I felt a force. My heart throbbed in time with the bass. His allure was consuming.

I reminded myself, *Stay present, Julie. This is a sacred moment. I am dancing with Baryshnikov! Make a note of this.*

I sensed he was predisposed to women falling for him. They danced with him, fell in love with him, and had his babies.

I still can't believe it actually happened. But there we were, all eyes upon us, suspended in time, on the dance floor.

Epilogue

I've been absolutely terrified every moment of my life and I've never let it keep me from doing a single thing that I wanted to do.
— Georgia O'Keeffe

NEARLY A DECADE SPENT MOSTLY IN PARIS (from 1983 to 1991) released my innate flamboyance and encouraged my ownership of it. I found that my cachet and mystique as a singer added up, giving me a more word-of-mouth credibility. (If she's happening in Paris, she's got to be good!)

Having studied Spanish in school, I had an understanding of Romance languages and applied that to learning French, which in turn helped me understand Paris and the French people. This cultural fluency inspired humorous stage patter between songs, influencing my audacious performance style.

From the American Embassy in Paris to the casino in Deauville, where the glitterati posed for the paparazzi, I was part of the scene.

A TV journalist from San Francisco, who visited Paris to do a feature on expat musical performers, led to my father finally acknowledging I was doing something of value in Paris. His friend called him from Frisco to say, "Hey, Sam, your daughter's on TV and in Paris! Why didn't you tell us?"

As the years went by, singing in Paris began to feel provincial. I realized in my sober maturity that America had much more to offer. When I was out of work in Paris, I was broke and nervous. But in the States, I found flexible employment as a teacher and there was always my devoted family if things became dire. I could create more freely in the States than in Paris. My command of French never got to an instinctual level. I stopped studying it once I could say the things I needed to say. That may have been the turning point in not choosing a life in Europe.

Now that I was a known entertainer, a world traveler, and something of a celebrity, I could launch a variety of performance opportunities in Seattle as well as in other fascinating places.

Finding myself dancing with Baryshnikov in Brussels had created a feeling that anything was possible.

I toured with a party circuit throughout France and England with Stacy Macadams and his group of singers. Though that was amusing, the lifestyle felt limited.

The Hollywood Savoy, after several incarnations under the same name, eventually changed ownership. Disneyland was soon to start expanding the entertainment industry in France, and the pending Euro currency transition promised all sorts of havoc that I had no patience for. Europe was being corporatized.

Back in Paris once more, I visited the American Church, not knowing it would be the last time. While I was perusing the church newspaper, an ad jumped out: "Looking for jazz singers to come to Istanbul." It was my ticket out of Paris. The next delicious adventure for this woman of the world was about to unfold.

Dress by Patrick Kelly
and Jerôme de Zilva Reid
Photo by Jerôme de Zilva Reid

Acknowledgements

My thanks go to: my dear friend Michael McCarthy, for generously helping me discover, streamline, and refine the language I needed to express my thoughts. And a special thanks to his patient and thoughtful husband David Rogers, who graciously let me borrow Michael for endless hours as we talked, argued, and laughed while working on my manuscript together.

C. Lee Sage, book doula, writer friend, and the first person to suggest and encourage me to tell my "interesting and valuable" story.

Jenn Hager, my first developmental editor, who loved everything I wrote and kept me busy for two years writing about everything.

Barb Bratlie, my devoted confidante since college, who saved every juicy letter and postcard I ever sent from Paris.

"Tor" for his empowering belief in my talent and his generosity of spirit that fueled my initial voyage to Paris and our lasting friendship.

John Engerman, longtime friend/designer/composer, who generously designed and laid out the book.

Mike Walker of the Hi Spot Café for his undying encouragement and sponsorship of my Facebook live show, the Pandemic Pick Me Up.

Jerry Lewis for his extensive and kind efforts ensuring my accurate use of French.

Cecille Miller, a friend willing to read my unedited manuscript and offer suggestions.

Stacy Macadams, the first musical director to take my talent seriously.

Bernard Brezet, my consultant for everything French.

Annette Lefebvre, kindred-spirited friend, who provided unlimited encouragement and multiple exquisite gifts for the body, mind, and spirit.

The Seattle Public Library, especially my favored branches, Wallingford and Greenwood, and the insightful, easygoing staff.

Carrie Wicks, dedicated proofreader, friend, and mentor.

Hugo House, where I found an inspiring community of fellow writers and Theo Nestor's developmental talents.

Nick Allison, the serious, detail-oriented final editor with a great sense of humor, who plays beautiful jazz piano for me sometimes.

Hedgebrook Foundation for their focus on and support of female writers.

Jack Straw Foundation for an artist support grant.

Heidi Kearsley, honorary member of my subconscious cheerleading crowd (You all know who you are!) consisting of patient, empathic listeners and people who may miss me when I disappear.

The late Ben Fleck, piano player extraordinaire, musical partner/collaborator, and sidekick for years before and after Paris.

Marilyn Michael, director of the writing group in the Wallingford Community Center, who indulged me by reading my chapters out loud to the class, which garnered helpful suggestions.

My brother Norman, role model and inspiration to follow an artistic career path.

My brother Tony, who comes through in surprising, loving ways when I least expect it.

Matthew Kangas for his generous consultations, and for unknowingly providing the title for my book.

Sam and Solveig Cascioppo, my always loving parents. Without them, there would be no me.

Author's Note

Everything I've written in this memoir is subject to the vagaries of memory. If I have misquoted, misinterpreted, or inadvertently slighted anyone, my apologies; please attribute it to the passage of time.

Certain time periods have been skipped over or combined to simplify the story, and some names have been altered for privacy purposes.

I hope my memories, journals, and letters have served their purpose.

. . . .

Designer's Note

Titles are set in Bauer Bodoni. The Bodoni typeface was originally designed at the end of the eighteenth century by Giambattista Bodoni, an Italian engraver, publisher, printer, and typographer. The Bauer Type Foundry version was drawn by Heinrich Jost in 1926.

The body text is set in Constantia, designed for Microsoft by John Hudson and released in 2004.

168/9   1987 Death of friend.

170 Palais Royale..
      remind me from
      Antoinette!

52-54 the Song Amsterdam!
63 - touch. cheeks!
64 — recipe.

43 Paris 1983.   65. Shoes her late 20's.

86 - Hollywood Savoy at the Bourse

97 - STACY — Yes.

105 - Payment method read 104/5

109 - New address check out google

read 110 - 111 useful info

119 oops her diary!! VIMA

read 130-131 She's NOT appealing
                           = to me.

nude publicity stunt 134
136 fawning?
151 femme fatale +MACE 153.
158 — interesting soulful observations
159 NICKS!!
174 Yes
181 — Her venues

Boyfriend ToR 80.

— 114 Her drinking
103 "Could I sit in" phrase VIMP

37 Chiv IF
14 Essentials on jazz
American church + Paris Cope 48

Printed in Dunstable, United Kingdom